Christmas 1976
To Rusty Spencer
from Oliver Goring
FDR Home, Hyde Park.

Presidents on Wheels

Presidents

PUBLISHED BY

on Wheels

by Herbert Ridgeway Collins
Associate Curator, The Smithsonian Institution

BONANZA BOOKS · NEW YORK

ILLUSTRATIONS ON TITLE PAGE:
Washington on his way to his first inauguration in 1789 as depicted in Harper's New Monthly Magazine, December 1888-May 1889, Vol. 78, p. 678.
Courtesy of the Smithsonian Institution

Carriage used by President Rutherford B. Hayes and later by President Garfield. Built by Brewster & Co., N.Y.
Courtesy of Rutherford B. Hayes Library

1961 "Stretch" Lincoln armored Limousine used by Presidents Kennedy, Johnson and Nixon.
Courtesy of the White House

Copyright © MCMLXXI by Herbert Ridgeway Collins
Library of Congress Catalog Card Number: 75-146-442
All rights reserved.
This edition is published by Bonanza Books
a division of Crown Publishers, Inc.
by arrangement with Acropolis Books
a b c d e f g h
Manufactured in the United States of America

Contents

viii/ List of Illustrations

x / Introduction

1
13 / George Washington

2
31 / John Adams

3
33 / Thomas Jefferson

4
38 / James Madison

5
43 / James Monroe

6
45 / John Quincy Adams

7
47 / Andrew Jackson

8
55 / Martin Van Buren

9
57 / William Henry Harrison

10
59 / John Tyler

11
63 / James K. Polk

12
65 / Zachary Taylor

13
69 / Millard Fillmore

14
73 / Franklin Pierce

15
77 / James Buchanan

16
79 / Abraham Lincoln

17
87 / Andrew Johnson

18
89 / Ulysses S. Grant

19
95 / Rutherford B. Hayes

20
97 / James A. Garfield

21
99 / Chester A. Arthur

22
101 / Grover Cleveland

23
106 / Benjamin Harrison

24
111 / William McKinley

25
119 / Theodore Roosevelt

26
129 / William H. Taft

27
137 / Woodrow Wilson

28
143 / Warren G. Harding

29
147 / Calvin Coolidge

30
153 / Herbert Hoover

31
155 / Franklin Roosevelt

32
171 / Harry S Truman

33
179 / Dwight D. Eisenhower

34
181 / John F. Kennedy

35
191 / Lyndon B. Johnson

36
195 / Richard M. Nixon

37
197 / White House Stables and Garages

205 / Bibliography

213 / Acknowledgements

215 / Index

List of Illustrations

The author with President Harry S Truman 5-20-66 / **page 11**

Pung sleigh used by George Washington on Christmas Day, 1776 / **page 12**

Powel coach at Mount Vernon / **page 17**

Washington on his way to his first inauguration in 1789 / **page 17**

Drawing of cypher for President Washington's chariot / **page 28**

Model of the Penn coach / **page 30**

Original panel from the Penn coach / **page 30**

Jefferson's design for his phaeton / **page 35**

President Jefferson's phaeton built at Monticello / **page 36**

Pleasure wagon used by President Monroe / **page 42**

Original panel showing "Old Ironsides" in full sail / **page 50**

President Jackson's phaeton made of wood from "Old Ironsides" / **page 50**

President Jackson enroute to Capital, 1829 / **page 51**

President Jackson's state coach / **page 52**

Carriage used by President Martin Van Buren / **page 54**

Carriage lamp from President Tyler's rockaway / **page 60**

President Tyler departing the Presidency / **page 61**

Drawing of President Polk's carriage / **page 64**

President Zachary Taylor mounted on "Old Whitey" / **page 67**

Carriage used by President Fillmore in Buffalo, N.Y. / **page 68**

Mrs. Fillmore's carriage / **page 71**

President Pierce's carriage and horses / **page 72**

President Pierce's two-wheeled chaise / **page 75**

President Buchanan's carriage built by Watson / **page 76**

President Buchanan's carriage built by Jacobs / **page 78**

President Lincoln's carriage at the Chicago Historical Society / **page 81**

President Lincoln's carriage built by Wood Brothers / **page 81**

President Andrew Johnson riding in his carriage, 1866 / **page 84**

President Grant's Arabian stallion / **page 87**

President Grant's carriage built by Wood Brothers / **page 88**

Carriage used by President Grant in Washington and New York / **page 92**

President Grant's children in the pony cart / **page 92**

Carriage used by Presidents Hayes and Garfield / **page 94**

Carriage used by President Garfield in Ohio / **page 96**

Victoria used by Presidents Arthur and Harrison / **page 100**

President Cleveland's landau built by Healey / **page 105**

President Cleveland's 1885 carriage / **page 106**

President Benjamin Harrison's buggy / **page 108**

Studebaker carriage used by President Benjamin Harrison / **page 108**

Studebaker carriage used by President McKinley / **page 110**

President McKinley's brougham, 1897 / **page 114**

Cabriolet used by President McKinley, 1897 / **page 114**

President McKinley's landau harness / **page 115**

Landau built for President McKinley, 1897 / **page 115**

President McKinley's hearse, 1901 / **page 117**

Brougham used by President Theodore Roosevelt / **page 118**

President Theodore Roosevelt's favorite riding horse / **page 121**

Victoria used by Presidents Roosevelt and Wilson / **page 121**

President Theodore Roosevelt enroute to the Capitol, 1905 / **page 122**

President Theodore Roosevelt's horses, harness and carriage / **page 122**

Mrs. Theodore Roosevelt's basket-type surrey / **page 125**

Phaeton used by President Theodore Roosevelt / **page 125**

President Taft's Baker electric / **page 128**

White steamer used by President Taft / **page 131**

Driver's Certificate issued to President Taft / **page 132**

President Taft's automobile, 1908 / **page 132**

Taft family and chauffeur in White steamer / **page 135**

Pierce-Arrow used by President Wilson / **page 136**

President and Mrs. Wilson in the victoria / **page 140**

Presidents Wilson and Harding enroute to inauguration, 1921 / **page 141**

Lincoln Cook car used by President Harding / **page 142**

President Harding in Florida, 1923 / **page 144**

President Harding in his Locomobile / **page 144**

President Harding in Washington / **page 145**

Official White House car of President Coolidge / **page 146**

Presidents Coolidge and Hoover enroute to the Capitol, 1929 / **page 148**

President Coolidge's academy carriage / **page 149**

1930 Cadillac purchased for President Hoover / **page 151**

Secret Service car, 1929 / **page 152**

"Sunshine Special" used by Presidents Roosevelt and Truman / **page 154**

President Roosevelt sleigh riding / **page 157**

Maxwell used by President Franklin Roosevelt in 1910 campaigning / **page 157**

President Roosevelt's 1936 Ford / **page 159**

1937 Lincoln used on the White House fleet / **page 159**

President Roosevelt with his 1932 Packard / **page 161**

1931 Plymouth used by President Roosevelt / **page 163**

President Roosevelt attending church in his 1933 Pierce-Arrow / **page 163**

President Roosevelt in his 1939 Packard / **page 164**

1933 Cadillac used by President Roosevelt / **page 164**

President Roosevelt in his 1936 Packard at New York World's Fair / **page 165**

President Roosevelt in Texas / **page 165**

President Roosevelt in England / **page 166**

President Roosevelt in Colorado / **page 166**

1932 Packard used by Franklin Roosevelt as Governor / **page 167**

President Roosevelt's chauffeur / **page 169**

1949 Lincoln used by President Truman / **page 170**

1950 Lincoln "Bubble Top" used by three Presidents / **page 170**

1939 "Sunshine Special" / **page 173**

Inaugural parade, 1949 / **page 174**

President Truman in the "Queen Mary" car / **page 174**

1940 Chrysler parade car / **page 177**

1942 Cadillac used by President Eisenhower / **page 178**

Inaugural parade, 1953 / **page 180**

President Eisenhower's honeymoon car / **page 180**

Lincoln Continental used by President Kennedy / **pages 183, 184, 187**

1961 Crown Imperial used by Mrs. Kennedy / **page 186**

Remodeled Lincoln Continental used by President Lyndon Johnson / **page 188**

FBI Director Hoover's car used by President Johnson / **page 190**

1961 "Stretch" Lincoln used by President Nixon / **page 193**

1968 "Stretch" Lincoln used by President Nixon / **page 193**

President and Mrs. Nixon in Ireland, 1970 / **page 194**

1967 Cadillac used by President Nixon / **page 196**

First White House stable, 1800 / **page 199**

1869 White House stables and horses / **page 199**

Interior of 1871 stable / **page 200**

1871 stable / **page 200**

1909 White House fleet / **page 201**

President's garage, 1916 / **page 202**

Interior of President's garage, 1916 / **page 202**

Demolition of White House stable, 1871 / **page 205**

President Theodore Roosevelt's harness room / **page 212**

President Theodore Roosevelt's saddles / **page 212**

White House baggage car, 1910 / **page 215**

Introduction

*T*raditionally, the Presidents' vehicles have not always been specially-built and armored-plated. In the beginning of our nation's history, many of the Presidents' carriages were not unlike those of other citizens traveling the streets of our cities.

Washington preferred a "neat genteel chariot" to the elegant state coach which had been bestowed upon Martha by the State of Pennsylvania. When notified of the appearance of one of his coaches, the first Chief Executive replied that he had rather that it be "plain and elegant than rich and elegant." John Adams preferred an elegant carriage to an ornate carriage and even insisted that Abigail dispense with putting the Quincy coat-of-arms on her carriage door, calling it a "trifling symbol of aristocratic pretension." A few of the Presidents, however, were an exception. Martin Van Buren rode through the streets of Washington adding a touch of grandeur with his ornate green state coach with its green-liveried coachman and footman and silver mounted harness.

The 20th Century changed all this. The need for securing the President from dissident or mentally-deranged persons has necessitated specially-built automobiles with added security features which have made the vehicles quite different from those of the ordinary citizen.

The cost, too, has greatly changed, so much so that the government has found it more economical to lease cars than buy them outright. This expenditure has not always been absorbed by the government. It wasn't until President Taft's Administration, that the government appropriated a set amount for the purchase of White House vehicles. Prior to that time, the President was expected to provide his own vehicles and horses. Many brought their own equipage and took it when they left the Presidency. Some accepted gifts of horses or carriages from influential friends or groups but in some cases their ethics were such that

they refused even this. President Andrew Johnson returned such an offer suggesting that it was not befitting a President to accept gifts. President Cleveland was so honest that he measured the hay in the stables when he assumed office and sent a check to Ex-President Arthur for it.

Some of our Presidents—Jefferson, Taylor, Grant and Theodore Roosevelt—preferred riding horses to riding in carriages. In some cases the transition from carriages to automobiles took time. President Theodore Roosevelt insisted on horse-drawn vehicles whenever possible and the "gas-less days" of World War I forced President Wilson to dig out the horse-drawn victoria.

Unlike vehicles associated with royalty and leaders in European countries, vehicles formerly used by our Presidents received little attention until recent years. When the Polk carriage was exhibited at the Columbian Exposition in 1893, it was in ruins and a disgrace to the dignity of the office it represented. A contemporary writer noted that it illustrated "how little we care for the possessions of those who have held high places" and "Who have passed from the stage of action and are forgotten." As a result no complete carriages exist for many of our early Presidents.

With the development of carriage and automobile clubs, greater interest has been shown in recent years which has made the writing of this book possible.

This study is an attempt to bring together all the known facts surrounding the vehicles our Chief Executives have used and what became of these vehicles. It is indeed surprising that at this late date as many vehicles as are represented in this study have survived.

There is no attempt made in this book to explore the rail, air and water transportation since that, in itself, would entail a separate and complete study.

—H. R. C.

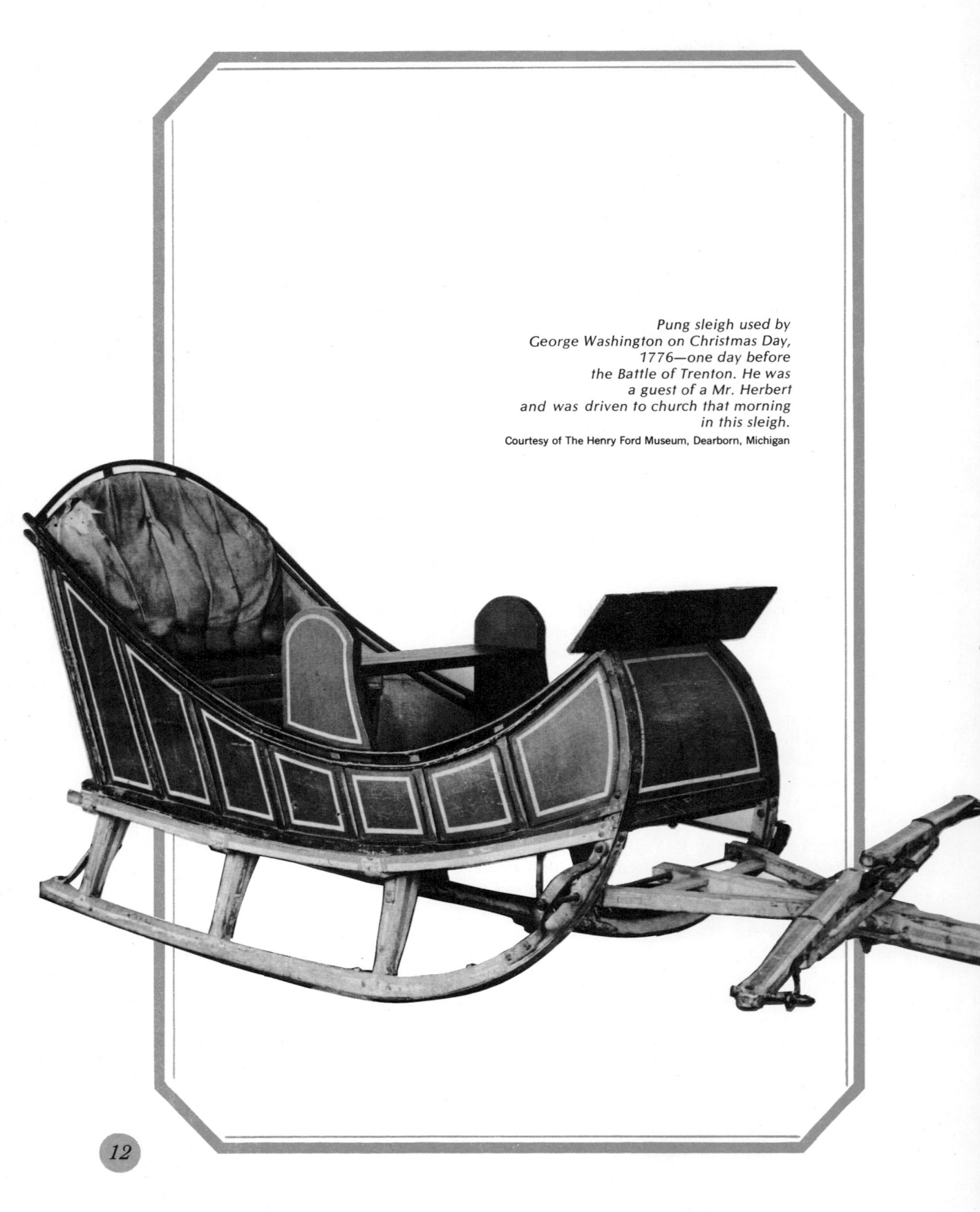

Pung sleigh used by George Washington on Christmas Day, 1776—one day before the Battle of Trenton. He was a guest of a Mr. Herbert and was driven to church that morning in this sleigh.
Courtesy of The Henry Ford Museum, Dearborn, Michigan

Chapter One

"I had rather have heard that
my repaired coach was plain and elegant
than rich and elegant."

George Washington

GEORGE WASHINGTON'S FIRST VEHICLE was a riding chair which he owned in 1750 when he was 18 years of age. His marriage to Martha Dandridge Custis in 1759 brought him into possession of another riding chair and a chariot which had belonged to her family. He must have disposed of one of the chairs by 1763, because in that year he paid taxes on a chariot and only one chair.[1]

The earliest instance of Washington's having a carriage made to order was not for himself but for Fielding Lewis, his brother-in-law. Record of this is found in a letter to Robert Cary and Company, dated March 16, 1762, requesting a "light Post Chariot for F.L. of a price not exceeding One hundred pounds Sterling and to have light Harness for Six Horses." It was to be "made of well Seasoned Wood and painted of a genteel and fashionable colour without any Arms." This chariot was sent to Colonel Lewis at Fredericksburg, Virginia; Lewis was to lodge a bill of exchange with Washington for the cost and charges.[2]

In 1768, Washington wrote Robert Cary and Company "My old chariot havg. run its race, and gone through as many stages as I could conveniently make it travel, is now rendered incapable of any further Service." He asked that they "bespeak him a new one." His specifications were that it be:

> *made in the newest taste, handsome, genteel and light; yet not slight and consequently unserviceable. To be made of the best Seasoned Wood, and by a celebrated Workman. The last Importation which I have seen, besides the customary steel springs have others that play in a Brass barrel, and contribute at one and the same time to the ease and Ornament of the Carriage; One of this kind there-*

13

fore woud. be my choice; and Green being a colour little apt, as I apprehend to fade, and grateful to the Eye, I woud. give it the pereference, unless any other colour more in vogue and equally lasting is entitled to precedency, in that case I woud. be governd by fashion. A light gilding on the mouldings that is, round the Pannels and any other Ornaments that may not have a heavy and tawdry look (together with my Arms agreeable to the Impression here sent) might be added, by way of decoration. A lining of handsome, lively col'd. leather of good quality, I sh'd also prefer; such as green, blue, or etc., as may best suit the col'r of the outside. Let the box that slips under Seat, be as large as it conveniently can be made (for the benefit of Storage upon a journey) and to have a Pole (not shafts) for the Wheel Horses to draw by; together with a handsome sett of Harness for four middle sized Horse ordered in such a manner as to suit either two Postilions (without a box) or a box and one Postilion. The box being made to fix on, and take off occasionally, with a hammel cloth etc., suitable to the lining. On the Harness let my Crest be engravd.[3]

Washington further observed that if such a chariot could be procured at a great savings that he would be obliged to have it.

In September 1768 the completed vehicle was shipped at a cost of £315.13.6 including transportation charges, from Christopher Reeves. This carriage was described as

a new handsome Chariot, made of best materials, handsomely carvd, carvd anticks to middle of Pillars, and carved scrowl Corners to top of Pillars and roof carvd with dble ribings, Batten sides, sweeps of Sides and mouldings rd. the roof carvd with dble ribings, hind battens and forebattens archd and carvd; panneld back and Sides Japand and Polishd, and roof Japand; lined wt. green Morocco Leather trimmed with Cuffoy Lace, an oval behind, a large Trunk under the seat, the bottom covrd with red leather and a handsome carpit to bottom: Plate Glass, diamd cut, handsomely Paintd, the Body and Carridge and whls. painted a glazd. green; all the framd Work of Body gilt, handsomely scrowl, shields, Ornamentd wt. flowers all over the Panls. body and Carridge Oil Varnished; the carridge wt. iron Axletree screwd at ends handsomely carvd scrowl Standds twisted behind and before, and stays of foot board barrs and beads carvd with scrowls and Panneled; Patent woorm Springs wt. brass sockets; a boot coverd wt. leather, Japand. and garnished, Brass nails, a hand. seat cloth, embroidered with bd. wt. brd. La. and 2 rows of hande. fringe wt. gimp head, all compt. 4 Venetian Patt. Blinds with Mahy. frames; 4 handsome harness briddles, brass Ornamt. pieces, on the Straps, brass arch'd Molden Housg. and Winkers, polisht. Bitts all compleat; 2 ridg. Sadles, stirps, and Girts; 2 Setts of Splinters and 2 main barrs wt. Ironwork; 4 high brass rings and 2 Waterg. hooks and Plates; a new covr. made of Green Bays; a strong deal case and casing up the Body."[4]

Within two years after delivery of the vehicle, Washington found it to be unsatisfactory and stated his complaint to the builder August 20, 1770, claiming that it was made of exceedingly green wood and that the panels had slipped out of the mouldings in the first two months of use and split from one end to the other and the joints opened so that the chariot was hardly serviceable.[5]

It was in this carriage that Washington traveled to the Continental Congress. Later, on June 19, 1775, Washington wrote from Philadelphia that he had sent his chariot and horses back to Mount Vernon for Martha's use, since he would not return until winter.[6]

On June 22, 1775, Washington bought a light phaeton from Peter Renaudet, a Philadelphia physician, and used it while in the Army. From a Mr. Todd, Washington bought a double set of harness for the phaeton.

In 1777 Washington gave Joseph Jones permission to use his phaeton at Philadelphia but refused to sell it.[7] The following year there is an account of Lund Washington selling the phaeton to George Lewis who in turn sold it to Mr. Jones for £300.[8]

Following his tenure as Governor of Pennsylvania (1771-1773), Richard Penn, Esq. returned to England in 1775. On June 14, 1777, the State of Pennsylvania purchased the handsome coach Richard Penn had left behind in America. A committee was established to purchase the coach for Martha Washington's use. On December 27, 1777, committee member William Coats, Esq. wrote from Lancaster, Pennsylvania, to David Rittenhouse, directing him to pay nine hundred and fifteen pounds, seventeen shillings on his delivery of a bill of exchange in the amount of purchasing £223.19.3 Sterling. The total price of the coach £457.18.6 was paid in two installments. Following is a description which appeared in the bill of sale:

Philadelphia 14th June 1777

The State of Pennsylvania to the Honble Richd.
Penn Esq. Dr.
For a very handsome round Bottom Crane Neck Coach made of the very best materials, the Bottom, Sides, Corner, Door Pillars, and Rails & Cornices Rails neatly run with raised Beads and fluted, Carved Anticks & raised Carved pieces to the tops of the Corner pillars, and jointed into the Cornices raised pieces on the tops of the Door pillars, neatly carved & ornamented with festoons of Carved Husts, the Beading of the Framework carved with Husks, the hollows fluted across and pearld, pannelld all the way up back and Sides, groved and cased all round for Glasses and Shutters, large Sweeps to the backs and sides, handsome festoons to the back & door rails and Doors neatly carved, fluted across and pearl'd, and a frettwork richly

carved all the top of the Cornice. A Rutland Roof covered with the best neats Leather and neat Vases on the Corner and Doorpillars, lined /line illegible/ best white belladine Silk Laces, glass strings, French Strings, Holders & check strings, the Seat Cloth with two Rows of white Gimpi beaded Fringe, and ornamented with green Silk Button Hangers, the fore and hind falls drawn up in Festoons and green Silk Footmans holders, the Tassell ornamented with white Silk Button hangers—The painting a pleasant Stone colour with four Seasons in Stone Colour upon a green ground, Copper within, neat ornamented brass oval in the large pannels; etc. and grotesque figures within ovals in the Side pannels; the beading of the frame Work moldings and festoons and ovals. the Springs Stays / Shackles and Body Loops all Gilt—The Roof Japand and polish'd plate Glasses all round. Mohagany Shutters Clamp'd covered with Neats Leather and lined with cloth to the fore hind / / and Sides, and green Silk Shutters to the Doors, the Steps within the / / and a carpet to the Bottom. A handsome Strong Carriage and Wheels with wrought brass cases and Strong /beaded/ moulding Cranes Suitable to the Body, the whole of the Carriage neatly run with Beads and hollows, the beds pannel'd cut through and Carved, the fore Standards made in imitation of an Orange Tree & Gretian foot board, with a Shield raised in the middle run and Carved, fixd under the foot board Stay. The hind Standards and Wings run twisted and Carved Scroles at the Bottoms and Vases Carved upon the Tops /levied/ up against the hind /one-half line omitted/ carriage carved with Husks and the hollows /one-half line omitted/ across, Iron'd with the best Town made eight square Iron work, Iron / /, with the best German Steel Springs, arms within the Shields painted under the footboards, and the Carriage and Wheels painted Stone colour the beading and Moulding of the Cranes and Iron Work Gilt and the fluting of the Hollows, pick'd out green and Varnish'd. The Body hung in the best green Neats Leather Main Cross and Collar Braces, Sewed white in portions. Welted with white Leather, Sewed green, the whole finished in the most Elegant and Workmanlike manner, with an handsome Embroidered Seat Cloth, the Ends forming Orange Trees, the Leaves in green Silk /painted with the Trunk of Gold finish/. the /top/ back and front of Superfine cloth trimmed with a handsome white Silk Lace and fringe, two Boards to fit the Ends; .... £362.

       Seat Cloth   21.

Two large Silk Squabb to the fore Ends and Hind & Squabbs to the Sides, the backs, Superfine green bound with white Silk Lace, Stuffd quilted and / / with Silk Tass .... 6.14.

A pair of spiral top Springs with green Silk Curtains /with/ Doors .... 1.12.

To polishing and varnishing by the best Artists in London   15.15.
A handsome pair of Town made Harnesses, made of the best Neats Leather, round Housings and Winkers with a pierced work of /Lutenague/ watering Hooks and Screw'd / / rings, four backpieces,

Courtesy of the Smithsonian Institution

Powel coach at Mount Vernon. Washington rode in this carriage when visiting the Powel family.

Courtesy of the Smithsonian Institution

Washington on his way to his first inauguration in 1789 as depicted in "Harper's New Monthly Magazine" December 1888-May 1889, Vol. 78, p. 678.

> Arch'd collar and /Breeching/ Straps welted with white Leather sewed green Serge wrought pieces.. £407.1
> Brought over   407.1
> Pieces upon the cruppers, and all the Straps ornamented with wrought pieces, Bredles, polish'd steel Bitts and Silk Reins compleat and two green Cloth pad Cloths /guarded/ with white cloth and Lined with Flannel... 43. ......
> A New Cover of the best green Baize 2.12.6
> Packing up the Body in a Strongdeal Case & packing the Carriage and Wheels in fine paper green Baize /   / in Matts & Hay / Banks/ .... 5.5 ......
> Sterling £ 457.18./6/
>
> One half... £ 228.19.3 [9]

An account of this coach appears in a travel diary of Robert Hunter, a young merchant of London, who visited Mount Vernon on November 17, 1785. The coach had been taken to Mount Vernon and remained there until after Washington was elected President, when it was moved to New York and later to Philadelphia. The Penn coach was left in Philadelphia when the Washingtons departed, and its disposition is described later in this chapter. Hunter's account of seeing the coach appears in his journal:

> After breakfast I went with Shaw to see his famous racehorse, a most beautiful creature. A whole length of him (Washington) was taken a little while ago, mounted on Magnolia, by a famous man from Europe, in copper, and his bust in marble one by order of Congress, to be kept wherever they sit, and the other by the State of Virginia, to stand in the House of Assembly. They will cost about six thousand sterling, Shaw says. He also showed me an elegant state carriage, with beautiful emblematical figures on it, made him a present by the state of Pennsylvania.
>
> I afterwards went into his stables, where among an amazing number of horses I saw old "Nelson," now twenty-two years of age, that carried the General almost always during the war. "Blueskin," another fine old horse next to him, now and then had that honor. Shaw also showed me his old servant, that was reported to have been taken with a number of the General's papers about him. They have heard the roaring of many a cannon in their time. "Blueskin" was not the favorite, on account of his not standing fire so well as venerable old "Nelson." The General makes no manner of use of them now; he keeps them in a nice stable, where they feed away at their ease for their past services. There is a horse of Major Washington's there that was reckoned the finest in the American Army.
>
> ... When the General takes his coach out he always drives six horses; to his chariot he only puts four. [10]

In his speech about the Washington Mansion in Philadelphia, an individual by the name of Nathaniel Burt stated that the most renowned of all Washington's coaches was a famous yellow one used in 1790 or 1791 and presented to Mrs. Washington by the Government of Pennsylvania.[11] Burt did not cite his authority for this statement, but it is obviously the Penn coach to which he was referring.

Several writers in modern times and particularly in the nineteenth century in referring to the Penn coach have mistakenly said it was presented to Washington by Louis XVI about 1790. The basis for that assumption is not known. It was probably in this coach, drawn by six white horses with a man on the box and a lackey on one of the wheelhorses, that Washington rode to the Hall of Congress accompanied by an escort of cavalry for his second inauguration in 1793. On that occasion he was driven by coachmen and footmen in off white livery trimmed with bright orange. A miniature model of the Penn coach used by J.L.G. Ferris in his paintings was for many years in the collections of the Franklin Institute of the State of Pennsylvania.

Pursuing another vehicle, Washington wrote to John Mitchell on March 20, 1780, inquiring about Pennsylvania coachmakers in Philadelphia or Germantown. His request specified "a genteel plain Chariot with neat Harness for four horses to go with two postilions." Five days later Mitchell replied describing "a Neat Genteel Chariot which is near finished . . . the price is Two Hundred and Ten pounds in Gold or the Value thereof in Current money" and could be available in two or three weeks, complete with harness.[12] At the end of that month, Washington approved the purchase at the stated price, provided Mr. Mitchell inspect it with a "critical eye" and be assured "that it is made in the present taste, well fashioned, composed of seasoned wood well put together and also that it either has, or is to have a proper lining etc."[13] Washington had been deceived in 1768 by Robert Cary and Company and almost was again in considering an elegant chariot of exquisite workmanship belonging to the Loyalist Captain Archibald Kennedy, because it turned out on second inspection to be too "old fashioned and uncouth." Washington was not to be misled again. He suggested that a General Dickenson—who was supposed to be in town—should also look at the proposed purchase, as he was a good judge. Washington also sent his arms and crest to be put on the vehicle should the deal materialize.[14] Mitchell recommended another vehicle owned by a Mr. Bringhurst, and on April 8, 1780, Washington wrote Mitchell that of the two chariots he had described, he preferred Bringhurst's as it was a better size. Washington's instructions were that the painting "be well done, and in a tasty stile with respect to color." He further wrote:

> Though I prefer a plain Chariot it may not be amiss to Ornament the Mouldings with a light airy gilting; this will add little to the ex-

pence and much to the appearance. The Harness I would have stout and strong, at the same time neatly made, Ornamented and of good leather. [15]

On April 15, 1780, Washington wrote to Lund Washington that he was having a chariot made in Philadelphia (meaning of course that being made by Bringhurst) at a price of 210 pounds in specie. It is possible that Washington later shipped this vehicle from Philadelphia to Mrs. George Augustine Washington.

In a letter to Mitchell, dated July 26, 1780, Washington refers to the money in Mitchell's hands from the sale of his old chariot, which apparently was the one which he had purchased from Robert Cary & Company in 1768. The amount of the sale is not mentioned.[16] Mr. Bringhurst, the coachmaker in Philadelphia who made the new vehicle, also bought the Cary chariot, according to a letter written to Mitchell by Washington in 1781. He directed that the balance of the money arising from its sale be paid to a Mr. Petit.[17]

When Washington went from Mount Vernon to New York in 1789, he rode in a post-chaise, a closed, four-wheeled carriage drawn by fast horses, which were changed at each post. This type of vehicle was most often hired by passengers for extended journeys. Upon his arrival in New York for the inauguration, long carpets were spread from the dock to the waiting carriage, but instead Washington preferred to go on foot from the dock to his residence on Cherry Street.

At New York, Washington kept from twelve to sixteen horses. The four used to draw the coach were cream-colored with white manes and tails, two were white chargers and the rest were handsome bays. The old chariot was again repaired at a cost of 17 pounds, along with the purchase of covers for the horses. With much patching and repairing, the chariot from Mount Vernon lasted only through his stay in New York. It was left behind and afterward sold for 45 pounds by Tobias Lear to Peter Kettletass, the builder of Bellevue on Manhattan Island.[18]

Washington's love of horses prevailed also in private life, and on one occasion the stables at Mount Vernon were enlarged to include a stall for Washington's war horse, "Nelson," the horse he had supposedly ridden in so many battles.

The practice of making gifts of horses or carriages to the Presidents had started even before we had a President when, on October 26, 1785, a jack and two jennets with a Spanish caretaker arrived at Boston, a gift to Washington from Charles III of Spain. Despite a prohibition against the exportation of full-blooded jacks from Spain, the King sent two as gifts for Washington, but only one survived the journey. Washington named the survivor "Royal Gift" and used it to breed heavy mules for draft pruposes. Lafayette also sent a Maltese jack which Washington named "Knight of Malta" and used to breed mules for saddle and carriage use.

Two entries appear in Tobias Lear's account book in July 1789 for the repair of Washington's vehicles. Both are paid to Robert Manly, one for repairing the coach at 34 pounds and the other for repairing the chariot at 28 pounds. Mr. Decatur, author of *Private Affairs of George Washington,* explains that at this time Washington was convalescing from an illness and that the coach was remodeled so he could lie on his side in it, and for several weeks was carried out to it every day for a ride around town with Mrs. Washington. [19]

When the nation's Capital was moved, Washington left his chariot in New York and rode to Philadelphia in the Penn coach. At Philadelphia, he rented a brick house from Robert Morris for $3,000 a year. Besides remodeling the house, Washington enlarged the stables to accommodate twelve horses. [20] Writing to Lear, September 5, Washington described the situation thus:

> *There is a room over the Stable (without a fireplace, but by means of a Stove) may serve the Coachman & Postillions. . . . There are good stables, but for 12 horses only a coach house which will hold my Carriages. . . .* [21]

The coach house held a state coach, a chariot, a phaeton, and a baggage wagon. Mr. Eberlein states in his study that:

> *whereas a private citizen could have got along quite comfortably and respectfully with a much smaller establishment, Washington felt it required every bit of what he maintained to uphold properly the dignity of his public office, no matter how burdensome the cost. His blooded bays, his famous white chargers, his hammer-cloth and the postillions' saddle cloths of leopard-skin trimmed with scarlet and gold braid, and his white or cream-colored liveries turned up with scarlet were essential that the equipage of the Chief Executive might not appear meaner in the eyes of the public than that of some of the wealthy citizens.* [22]

After Washington had put the Morris House and stables in order suitable to his tastes and needs, he turned his attention to the carriages. His official state carriage, the continental chariot, was sold in New York on September 30 for 45 pounds and Washington credited the United States Government in his books. Although the price was not enough, Washington approved the sale because it could eliminate further storage cost, and he summed it up in these words: "The Sale of the old Chariot was proper for although the price is small it will be so much saved for the public." [23]

On September 9, 1790, Washington wrote to Lear concerning harness which was being made by Clark, the Philadelphia coachmaker on Chestnut Street. The harness was to be plated and handsomely executed. It should include harness for the pole-end, in addition to that for the wheel horses, and was to be ready by the middle of November.

Besides engaging the Clark brothers (David and Francis) to furnish him with harness, Washington also engaged them to restore Martha's coach, the one which had belonged to Penn. The following list of repairs and estimate was sent to Washington by the Clarks on September 13, 1790:

REPAIRS FOR THE COACH (PENN) [24]

Taking out the Creans and reasing higher & a pair of new Shafts	£7.10.0
A new iron Coach box Sett	3.15.0
A new Ruff Leather & new Conish	4.12.6
Linning the Boady with 11½ yards of Superfine Cloath at 37/6 pr. yard	21.11.3
Laces Glass string etc.	8.14.0
Making and putting in Do.	8.10.0
A new fulle trimed hamer Cloath	12.0.0
repairs wanted to the boady & 2 pair of new hinges	2.0.0
A pair of new double inside foulding Steps	5.10.0
Boarder rond all the pannels from £8. to £115	
Ornaments & Coats of Arms	4.10.0
Guilding the frame work Solid	6.0.0
Painting Carriage and wheels	2.10.0
Picking in Do	1.10.0
8 Vinisen blinds	22.10.0
Gilding the Springs	2.5.0
A sett of Silke festoon Curtains with fringes and tasals to all the inside of the Ruff	8.0.0

In answer to the letter of September 13 from the Clarks, which enclosed not only the list of repairs and estimate, but also the draft of a cypher, Washington gave the following specifications in his reply dated September 17, 1790:

The colour is to be as at present; but to be neatly painted and highly varnished.... The Seasons (which are now on the carriage) is to be continued on the doors, front and back—and my crest without any cypher is to be on the four quarter pannels; all to be enclosed with the original ovals—If it is thought best that the crests should be painted (as Silver does not show on a light ground) they may be painted—But   , whether if some ornamental painting within the Oval, and around the Silver crests (the colours of which should form a contrast to the silver and not be inconsistent with other parts of the work) might not look well. This is only suggested, for you may have painted, or silver crests put on according to your own judgment of the propriety & uniformity.... The Seasons (if they should require it and a masterly hand can be employed) must be repaired, or at least freshened in their appearance to make them correspond with the fresh painting of the Coach & as festoons were on the coach before might they not be there again if the seasons etc. are retained. . . . I approve of the patern sent as lining for the coach and desire you may use it. . . . Plated handles to the doors . . . plated brace buckles, and plated mouldings around the roof should be added to make one part correspond with the other. A Glass in front must unquestionably be provided. . . . In all other respects you are to observe the directions which was given when I saw you in Philadelphia. [25]

The ground color of the coach was white.

Washington then wrote to Tobias Lear in November 1790 informing him as follows:

I have left my Coach to receive a thorough repair against I return (which I expect will happen before the first of December) and I request you will visit Mr. Clark (into whose hands it is committed) often, to see it well done; and that I may not be disappointed in the time allowed him for completion, which is by the 25th of November. The harness is also left with him, and he has my Ideas on this subject:—generally they are, if the wheel harness (which I understand was left at New York) can be made complete, and look as well as if they were new, then & in that case, he is to make a set of pole-end Harness to suit them, both to be plated—but if this cannot be accomplished, the set is to be made entirely new,—and in the best style.

A coach and four was hired for the rest of the journey and arrangements made for it to bring the family back to Philadelphia later. [26] At a second interview with Clark, it was decided to make all the harness entirely new and later the President added to it to allow for six horses, his instructions to that effect to Lear, on November 17, reading:

As the addition of a pair of leading Harness to the Coach will not greatly enhance the aggregate cost, I wish, in order that the whole may be of a price, that you would order Clarke to make a sett for the two leaders (with a Postillion Saddle, the Saddle cloth of which to be the same as the Hammel Cloth with the same lace) that I may have Harness alike for Six Horses when the Coach is used—with that number. [27]

Washington made a slip of the pen in the word hammel. He should have written hammer, a hammercloth being the covering for the coachman's box. This and the saddle cloths were of leopard skin, trimmed with red and gold lace.

When Lear informed Washington that the restored coach was rich and elegant, Washington replied with the statement that he "had rather have heard that" his "repaired Coach was plain and elegant than rich and elegant." [28]

The coach recieved a new coat of paint, was reupholstered, its metal trim re-plated and its harness replaced. It was a very handsome coach and really looked like a "coach of state" but it was too heavy and elegant for hard use on the roads. A lighter vehicle was needed for such travel and, accordingly, Washington ordered the Clarks to build the one which eventually became confused with the Powel coach. The estimate for this chariot was given to Washington on September 13, 1790. The new chariot was painted a cream color and was trimmed to match the Penn coach.

David Clark brought from England two new vehicles, one of which was sold to George Washington, as earlier stated, and the other to Mrs. Samuel Powel, wife of the Mayor of Philadelphia. Washington's Philadelphia account book shows three different payments totaling $389.63 made to Messrs. David and Francis Clark during June and July 1793 for the President's phaeton. This coach built by the Clarks is most often described as the "White Chariot." After the death of General Washington, the chariot and harness was purchased for $610.00 by G.W.P. Custis from the executors for his own use. The last owner was a Virginia clergyman, Bishop Meade, who broke it up and distributed the pieces as souvenirs among admirers of the first owner. These pieces, made into souvenirs, were sold at church fairs and other charitable occasions. Of this vehicle, the Bishop writes:

> *His old English coach (misused term for chariot), in which himself and Mrs. Washington not only rode in Fairfax county, but travelled through the entire length and breadth of the land, was so faithfully executed, that at the conclusion of that journey, its builder, who came over with it, and settled in Alexandria, was proud to be told by the general, that not a nail or screw had failed. It so happened, in a way I need not state, that this coach came into my hands about fifteen years after the death of General Washington. In the course of time, from disuse, it being too heavy for these latter days, it began to decay and give away. Becoming an object of desire to those who delight in relics, I caused it to be taken to pieces and distributed among the admiring friends of Washington who visited my house, and also among a number of female associations for fairs and other occasions, made a large profit by converting the fragments into walking-sticks, picture-frames, and snuff-boxes. About two-thirds of one of the wheels thus produced one hundred and forty dollars. There can be no doubt that at its dissolution it yielded more to the cause of charity than it cost its builder at its first erection. Besides other mementoes of it, I have in my study, in the form of a sofa, the hind seat, on which the general and his lady were wont to sit.* [29]

This coach is mentioned in the memoirs of G.W.P. Custis and was described as "handsome, genteel and light." [30]

The steps to this chariot are now at Mount Vernon, as well as a piece of a door panel and a cane made from one of the wheel spokes. The door panel is approximately one foot square. It was presented by Bishop Meade to Reverend

Bolton of Pelham, New York, and was purchased from his daughter, Miss Adele Bolton, by Mrs. Elizabeth L. Broadwell, for Mount Vernon. Another cane made from a spoke appeared in the collection of A.B.W. Cooke in 1935.[31]

President Washington made his southern tour in 1791 in this carriage. A contemporary newspaper stated that Washington was starting South "in a new chariot and six . . . built by Mr. Clark . . . a superior specimen of mechanical perfection."[32] Washington's diary mentions only four horses, saying:

> *In this tour I was accompanied by Major Jackson,—my equipage and attendance consisted of a Chariot and four horses drove in hand—a light baggage Wagon and two horses—four saddle horses besides a led one for myself—and five—to wit;—my Valet de Chambre, two footmen, Coachmen and postilion.*[33]

John Fagan, the Hessian coachman, drove for the President throughout the tour. James Hurley was postilion and riding beside the carriage was Washington's Secretary, Major Jackson. Also mounted were John Mauld and the valet, William Osborne. Giles drove the baggage wagon with two horses and Paris rode horseback at the rear of the group leading the President's old white charger. Attending the President were Thomas Jefferson and Henry Knox.[34]

Since Washington would have to leave several horses in Philadelphia for Mrs. Washington to use while he was on the tour, he purchased three additional horses from William Davidson. Two of these he took with him and during the trip he wrote Lear that they were "much worn down" and did not measure up to his standards.

After Washington returned from his southern tour, David Clark called on him to inspect the condition of the chariot after such a hard trip and proudly listened while the President remarked on the excellence of his workmanship. Not a screw or bolt had come loose.[35]

Of the two coaches built by the Clark Brothers, only the Powel coach survived. For many years it was erroneously said to be Washington's. One of the earliest such claims appeared in the periodical *Drawing-Room Companion* of November 4, 1854, page 281. Here an engraving of the coach is reproduced with the following caption: "the engraving given below represents the veritable carriage formerly belonging to Washington. It was left by the general to Elizabeth Powel, since which time it has come into the hands of John Ham Powel, Esq. of Philadelphia, nephew of Elizabeth. It has not had horses harnessed to it for forty years, and is now in perfect order." Mrs. Beall, in her study, claims that the Powel family did at one time own a Washington carriage, and it probably fits the story of that one which the general left to Elizabeth Powel, and which later fell to pieces through old age.

The Powel coach was exhibited as Washington's coach at the Centennial Exposition of 1876 and attracted much attention. The coach was later purchased by the Michigan Vice-Regent of Mount Vernon in 1901, and placed in the carriage house at Mount Vernon as George Washington's coach. By this time it had been proven not to be Washington's, but rather its counterpart, the Powel coach—ordered, built, and imported at the same time. Thus, it is of the period of the Washington vehicle and is a most fitting substitute in the coach house at Mount Vernon.

Washington's accounts disclose that he paid a Mr. Page in July and October of 1792, seven dollars a day for 22 days' use of Page's carriage, horses and driver for trips to Mount Vernon. Mr. Decatur in his study asserts that Washington, instead of driving his Penn coach to Mount Vernon, would use Mr. Page's vehicle whenever possible, unless, sometimes in a hurry, he would make the entire journey on horseback. The Penn coach, with its elegant cream-colored paint and art panels would have been covered with dust or mud and thus ruined. Decatur describes Washington's riding habits in this way: "Washington usually sat almost silently in the coach with the family, but occasionally would mount one of his chargers, which was always taken along for the purpose, and ride beside the coach as a means of breaking the monotony of the journey."[36]

The coach mentioned in Mrs. Beall's study claimed to have been Washington's coachee and Martha's favorite, was sold at Thomas' auction rooms of Philadelphia in 1892 to a circus company which later sold it to Barnum and Bailey. In 1894 Robert Brownfield of Philadelphia purchased it and deposited it at Mount Vernon where it remained on exhibition until 1901. It was returned to Mr. Brownfield in 1905, leaving the Powel coach on exhibition at Mount Vernon. The coachee was later presented to the United States National Museum where it remains today.

The coachee was built for everyday use and was of lesser elegance than any of the vehicles which Washington possessed. The coach was strongly built with springs of wood and could have been drawn by two horses. The body, painted a warm shade of claret, is a nice contrast to the lining and cushions which are tan. The seat is on hinges, being divided in the middle and folding back against the sides so as to allow the rider to enter by use of a rear door, a feature not common in a coachee.

Some historians have for many years regarded this vehicle as the only authentic Washington vehicle in existence, but recent investigations tend to disprove or at least discount that theory (D. H. Berkebile: "A Statement Concerning the Proof of the Washington Coachee"). Much of the documentation regarding the coachee was based on a tradition and recollections of individuals who had once known of a so-called "Washington coachee." The vehicle which is now in the United States National Museum was not referred to as a "coachee" until after 1894. Former owners had designated it variously as a carriage, coach, or gig. A coachee usually had side doors, while this one has a back door. Mr. Berkebile, in the Smithsonian's Division of Transportation, feels that the vehicle in the national collection is more like a "Jersey wagon" than a "coachee."

Washington owned two carriages to which he applied the term coachee. One was purchased in 1793 from George Way at a cost of $192.66, and the other in 1795 from Walter Johnson at a cost of $336.42.[37] One of these two was sold July 21, 1802, after Martha's death to Charles Carter, Betty Washington Lewis' son-in-law, who lived near Culpeper, Virginia. The coachee and harness brought $250.00. Mr. Carter later moved to the vicinity of Danville, Virginia, and nothing more is known of this coachee.[38]

On December 28, 1913, a photograph of a two-horse shay appeared in the *New York Times*. The shay was then owned by Walter Scott of Cheshire, Connecticut, who claimed that George Washington had ridden in it. No further reference to this vehicle has been found.

A most interesting vehicle associated with Washington is a pung sleigh in which he was supposed to have ridden to church on Christmas Day, December 25, 1776, one day before the battle of Trenton. Washington was a guest of a Mr. Herbert. The sleigh later came into the family of William C. Crosby of Poughkeepsie, New York, who in 1928 gave it to The Henry Ford Museum and Greenfield Village, where it remains today. Made in Red Bank, New Jersey about 1750, the sleigh was first owned by John Ludwig, a German, who had a farm between Trenton and Princeton and was the father of the celebrated "Molly Pitcher" (Molly Ludwig).

Washington's integrity prevailed even when it came to hiring a sorely-needed coachman. On March 22, 1789, George Mason's coachman applied to Washington. He refused to hire him until he had first checked with Mason as to whether he was agreeable to the arrangement.[39]

There is an old description of 'Dutch John' or 'Fritz,' as this coachman (John Gaceer) was generally called, which gives a very good idea of his appearance. It says he was a tall, muscular German, with an aquiline nose; he wore a cocked hat, square to the front, seemingly in imitation of his principal but

Drawing of a cypher suggested by the Clarks for President Washington's chariot.

thrown a little back upon his long cue, and presenting to the memory a figure "not unlike that of Frederick of Prussia, upon the sign in Race Street"; he exhibited an important air, and was obviously proud of his charge.[40]

Only a few pieces of the many vehicles owned by George Washington have survived the ravages of time. A panel from the Penn coach of 1771, remodeled by the Clarks in 1790, is today in the United States National Museum and bears on the reverse side the inscription: "This painted copper plate was taken from the state coach belonging to Genl. G. Washington when President of the U.S. of America. Identified by Genl. G.W.P. Custis. Deposited by John Varden." The back of the panel is inscribed in ink: "This Plate and Painting was on a Coach once belonging to George Washington and given to John Varden Proprietor of the Washington Museum about the year 1838 by Mrs. Mary Dunlap of Pha." The quarter panels were ornamented with the four seasons, the originals of which were painted by Caprini, an Italian painter of the 18th century who lived and worked mostly in Rome. The panel in the United States National Museum is painted with cupids and flowers representing spring.

---

1 Taxes levied on Daniel Custis, April 7, 1758, *Writings of Washington*, Vol. 2, p. 390.
2 Ford, *Writings of Washington*, Vol. 2, p. 374.
3 *Ibid.*, Vol. 2, pp. 488-490.
4 *Ibid.*, Vol. 2, pp. 488-490.
5 *Ibid.*, Vol. 37, p. 493.
6 *Ibid.*, Vol. 3, p. 298.
7 *Facsimile of Washington's Account Book during the War.*
8 *Letters of Joseph Jones of Virginia 1777-1787*, pp. 2, 3, 4.
   Ford, *Writings of Washington*, Vol. 9, pp. 232, 233.
9 *Writings of Washington*, Vol. 12, p. 328.
10 *Quebec to Carolina in 1785-1786.*
11 *Annals of Philadelphia*, Vol. 2, p. 276.
12 Penn Papers, Pennsylvania Historical Society.
13 *Ibid.*
14 Ford, *Writings of Washington*, Vol. 12, p. 328.
15 *Ibid.*, Vol. 18, pp. 177-178.
16 *Ibid.*, Vol. 18, pp. 177-178.
17 *Ibid.*, Vol. 18, pp. 233-234.
18 *Ibid.*, Vol. 19, p. 253.
19 *Ibid.*, Vol. 21, p. 249.
20 *Ibid.*, Vol. 37, p. 571.
21 Letter Book, George Washington Papers, Library of Congress, *Transactions of the American Philosophical Society*, Vol. 43, Part 1, p. 164.
22 Ford, *Writings of Washington*, Vol. 31, p. 154.

23 Washington's Household Account Book 1793-1797, *Pennsylvania Magazine of History and Biography*, Vol. XXIX, No. 4.
24 *Ibid.*
25 *Washington's Diary*, Vol. 4, p. 149.
26 Decatur, *Private Affairs of George Washington*, pp. 162-163.
27 *Ibid.*, pp. 162-163.
28 Ford, *Writings of Washington*, Vol. 31, p. 154.
29 *The Gazette of the United States,* March 23, 1791, p. 3.
30 *Washington's Diary*, Vol. 4, p. 149.
31 *Hobbies,* A Magazine for Collectors, May 1935, p. 10.
32 *The Gazette of the United States,* Mar. 3, 1791, p. 3.
33 Meade, *Old Churches, Ministers and Families of Virginia,* Vol. 2, p. 237.
34 *Annual Report 1950,* The Mount Vernon Ladies' Association, p. 21.
35 Decatur, *Private Affairs of George Washington,* pp. 162-163.
36 Decatur, *Private Affairs of George Washington,* p. 290.
37 Philadelphia Account Book, pp. 42, 57, 55, 473.
38 Inventory of Washington estate.
39 Ford, *Writings of Washington,* Vol. 30, p. 249.
40 Decatur, *Private Affairs of George Washington,* p. 282.

Original panel painted by Caprini for the Penn Coach.

Courtesy of Smithsonian Institution

Model of the Penn coach by J. L. C. Ferris.

Courtesy of Smithsonian Institution

Chapter Two

"My chariot is finished,
and I made my first appearance in it yesterday.
It is simple, but elegant enough."

John Adams

EVEN BEFORE THE OFFICIAL VOTE was tallied, a foremost thought of John Adams was to acquire a carriage and horses fitting for the United States President. In calculating costs, however, he was astonished that "a common chariot of the plainest sort could not be bought for less than six hundred dollars."[1]

Whereas Washington's six-horse carriage was elegant, Adams used only two horses and preferred not to "excite popular feelings and vulgar insolence for nothing."[2] When his wife, Abigail, expressed a desire to have the Quincy coat-of-arms painted on her carriage door, he denounced the idea as a "trifling symbol of aristocratic pretension" and vetoed the idea. The Adams' coach horses were named Caesar and Cleopatra.

When John Adams became President on March 4, 1797, he moved directly into the Philadelphia residence formerly occupied by George Washington. In a letter to his wife, two days later, John Adams wrote: "It is now settled that I am to go into his (Washington's) house. It is whispered that he intends to take French leave tomorrow. I shall write you as fast as we proceed. My chariot is finished, and I made my first appearance in it yesterday. It is simple, but elegant enough. My horses are young, but clever."[3] An earlier letter, dated February 4, 1797, to Abigail stated that the house rent was $2,700 a year, the carriage cost $1,500, and the horses $1,000 a pair. He also declared his intention to keep only one pair of horses for a carriage and one horse for a saddle.[4]

The Presidential Mansion in Washington was still under construction when the First Family moved in during November, 1800, and on the 21st Abigail wrote to her daughter: "The house is on a grand and superb scale, requiring about thirty servants to attend and keep the apartments in proper order, and perform the ordinary business of the house and stables."[5]

In a letter of November 25, 1800, Mrs. Adams mentioned a coachman at the White House,[6] but her husband had dispensed with the marshals, guard of honor, and ornate carriage of George Washington. John Adams preferred an elegant chariot to an ornate carriage. An inventory taken on February 27, 1801, showed that the stables of the new President's house contained "7 well looking horses, chiefly advanced in years, 1 Sett brass Do. for four Horses, 1 Elegant Chariot, 1 Good Coachee, 1 Saddle & Holsters and 1 Market Waggon."[7]

Adams refused to ride with his successor, Thomas Jefferson, to the inauguration in 1801. Instead he left Washington, D.C. at daybreak in his coach for the 500-mile, 14-day journey to Boston.[8]

No coaches used by either John Adams or his son, John Quincy Adams, are now in existence, although the Adams' carriage house at Quincy, Massachusetts still stands.

---

[1] Smith, *John Adams,* p. 908.
[2] *Ibid.,* p. 923.
[3] Seward, *Life of John Quincy Adams,* p. 69.
[4] *Ibid.,* p. 67.
[5] Singleton, *The Story of the White House,* Vol. 1, pp. 11-13.
[6] *United States Magazine,* Vol. III.
[7] Record Group 128 (Senate) 6th Congress "Report of the Joint Committee on the President's Message of the 16th inst. Relative to Public Property in His Hands." Legislative Branch, The National Archives.
[8] Martin, *After the White House,* p. 33.

Chapter Three

A lover of horses, Jefferson was known to have ridden horseback as much as 40 miles a day. Five days after leaving office, he mounted his horse and rode 140 miles to his home at Monticello.

Thomas Jefferson

THOMAS JEFFERSON WAS A GREAT ADMIRER of fine horses. He enjoyed being on horseback and usually rode a favorite horse around his plantation each day, sometimes for distances up to forty miles.[1] One of many accounts of Jefferson's horse purchases concerned "Wildair," a 7-year-old bay which he bought from Colonel John Hoomes of Bowling Green, Virginia in 1801. "Wildair" stood 16 hands high and cost Jefferson $300.[2]

Although few details are known about vehicles owned by Jefferson, his farm book entries indicate that he possessed many.[3] In 1773, for example, he paid taxes on one chariot and one phaeton, but the next year only on a phaeton. In 1782 he had a chariot and one chair; in 1788, he purchased a new Crane Neck chariot and four sets of harness; in 1800 he had one phaeton. From Conrad Hanse, Jefferson bought a chariot in 1801. It was complete with harness for four horses and two postillion saddles. He kept it until 1809, when he sold it to a Dr. Elzey.

The farm book also indicates that Jefferson owned carriages outside of his home county. During his service in France he was constantly seeking the latest objects—among which were several beautiful carriages—for his American home. A 1791 Farm Book entry list Jefferson's payment to J. Ross for freight on his carriages from LeHavre. In 1794, his entry referred to taxes paid to Thomas Diverson on "my phaeton, the only carriage I have in this county."

Like most of Jefferson's furnishings at Monticello, his vehicles bore the touch of his ingenuity. Most of the wheelwrights who built his carriages and gigs, his landau, phaetons, carts, and wagons lived at Monticello. They were assisted by Monticello smiths, who fashioned iron parts for the vehicles.

The phaeton which is today exhibited at Monticello was made there around 1805 from Jefferson's own design. A copy of this design was sent to J. P. Reibelt that October. The original design is now in the Alderman Library, University of Virginia, Charlottesville, Virginia. According to Thomas Jefferson Randolph IV, Jefferson's great, great grandson, the inlay on this phaeton was made by Louis A. Leschot, a Swiss watchmaker who came to Albemarle County, Virginia, and is buried at Monticello. The phaeton remained at Monticello, was acquired by the Thomas Jefferson Memorial Foundation with the estate in 1923, and was restored by the generosity of Whitney Stone in 1950. This phaeton was erroneously identified as the gig in which Jefferson rode to Philadelphia to present his draft of the Declaration of Independence. In 1926, this vehicle, mounted on a white automobile chassis with an armed escort and accompanied by officials of Virginia and the American Automobile Association, was one of the highlights of the Sesqui-Centennial Exposition in Philadelphia.[4]

There are several entries in the farm book regarding repairs to Jefferson's vehicles. In 1803, he paid Jones and Kain for completing a phaeton, for wheels which he used on the market wagon, and for repairs made to harness. In 1814 he purchased scarlet rattinett for use in lining his carriage.[5]

Jefferson had no carriage of his own when he arrived in Washington for his inauguration in 1801. He had sent to Virginia to order a coach and four from Jack Eppes, but poor road conditions prevented their timely delivery.[6] There have been many published descriptions of Jefferson's ride to the Capitol on his white horse, but they seem to have little basis in fact. Actually, Jefferson was lodging at the former residence of Thomas Law, which had been made into apartments belonging to the Messrs. Conrad and McMunn. The house on New Jersey Avenue, S.E., known as the Law House and later as The Varnum was only about 100 yards from the Capitol,[7] so he probably walked to the inauguration. On the other hand, he probably did ride horseback in 1805 for his second inauguration, and the various accounts may have confused the 1801 and the 1805 inaugurations. According to reports in the *National Intelligencer,* "at 12 o'clock Thomas Jefferson, attended by a number of his fellow-citizens, among whom were many members of Congress, repaired to the Capitol . . . after which he returned to his lodgings, accompanied by the Vice-President, Chief Justice, and heads of Departments." Jefferson stayed for two weeks at the Law House before moving into the Executive Mansion.

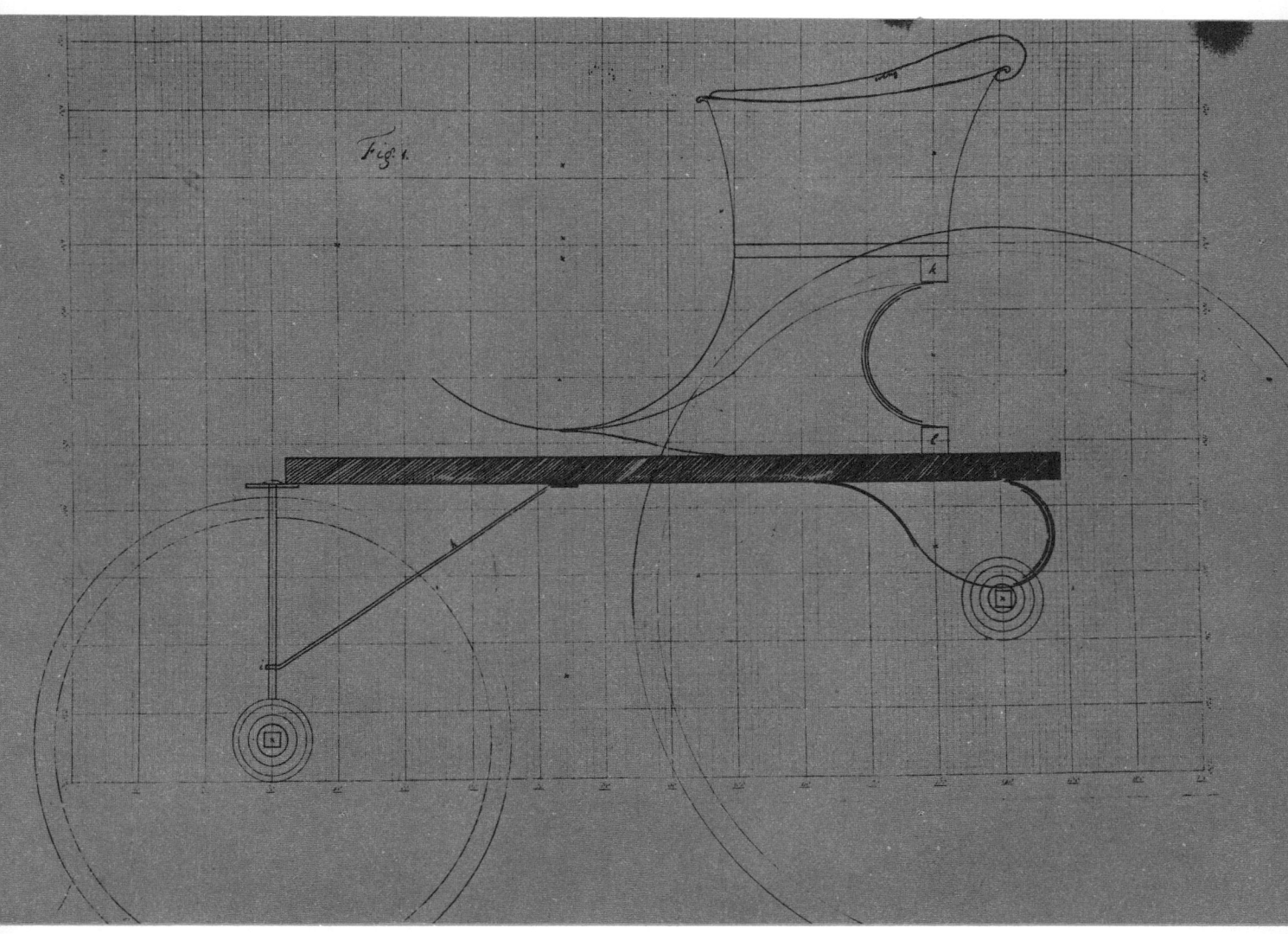

One of three original drawings of the phaeton was designed by Thomas Jefferson. The original drawings are now in the Alderman Library of the University of Virginia.

Phaeton designed by Thomas Jefferson and built at Monticello. The seat and body are original; the wheels have been replaced.

Courtesy of the Thomas Jefferson Memorial Foundation

Little is known about carriages Jefferson used during his stay in the White House. During his Presidency he purchased from Conrad Hanse for $1,200 a "new plain, well-furnished chariot with plated harness for 4 horses and 2 postillion Saddles."[8] Whether he bought this equipage for use at the White House or at Monticello is not certain. Since Jefferson was a widower with no family when he went into the White House, he felt no need for an elaborate coach. He usually rode his favorite horse on both official and unofficial business.[9]

When Jefferson moved to the White House in 1801, his horses were stabled at the southeast corner of 14th and G Streets, N.W. Some years later this building was converted into a school. As a new abode for his horses, Jefferson had a temporary stable, cowshed, and carriage barn constructed on the Treasury side of the White House grounds.[10][11] This building was designed to aesthetically balance the office building constructed in 1806 on the west side of the White House. The foundations of these Jeffersonian outbuildings were uncovered during the Theodore Roosevelt renovations.

Although Jefferson rode to his 1805 inauguration on horseback, he returned in a carriage, setting a precedent for inaugural parades along Pennsylvania Avenue to the White House.[12]

When Jefferson left the White House in 1809, he declined Madison's invitation to drive to the Capitol in the Presidential coach, saying that he did not want to divide the honors.[13] He did, however, accompany his successor to the inauguration, riding in a separate carriage escorted by cavalry troops. Five days after the inauguration, Jefferson mounted his horse and made his way through the snow and sleet to private life and his beloved home at Monticello, 140 miles away.[14]

---

[1] Martin, *After the White House,* p. 70.
[2] Thomas Jefferson Papers, Jefferson's Household Account Book, 2 Vols. (Library of Congress).
[3] Betts, *Thomas Jefferson's Farm Book,* p. 460.
[4] *The Spokesman and Harness World,* July 1926, Vol. 42, p. 21. Austin, *The Sesqui-Centennial International Exposition,* pp. 128, 170, 380.
[5] *Ibid.*
[6] *Ibid.*
[7] Willets, *Inside History of the White House,* p. 433.
[8] Clar, *Biographical Sketch of Thomas Law,* p. 25.
[9] Thomas Jefferson Papers. Correspondence between Enoch Edwards and Jefferson.
[10] *American Motorist,* March 1933, Vol. 25, p. 6.
[11] Roberts, *Washington, Past and Present,* p. 54.
[12] Hurd, *The White House,* p. 34.
[13] *New York Journal,* Jan. 11, 1957. Hurja, *History of Presidential Inauguration,* p.19.
[14] Leupp, *Walks Around Washington,* pp. 132-133.
[15] Martin, *After the White House,* pp. 53, 55.

Chapter Four

His wife blossomed out in rich clothes and queened about the city in her coach and four which cost $1,500.

James Madison

ONE OF THE EARLIEST CARRIAGES used by the Madisons is that mentioned as having been locked in his coach house in Washington in 1802. The chariot was of "neat plain elegance," with silver-plated harness. It was glassed all around with Venetian blinds, and a light-colored cloth interior with lace trim. The wheels were boxed and the coachman's seat was in a circular form. The two doors carried the monogram "M" in silver. The lamps on either side held candles. The carriage was built in Philadelphia at a cost of $594.00.[1]

The Madisons arrived for the Inaugural Ball of 1809 in their handsome coach drawn by four horses with a Negro coachman and footmen.[2] During their first year in the White House, the noted architect Benjamin F. Latrobe designed and built a carriage house near the stables constructed during Jefferson's term of office.[3]

Mrs. Madison promptly asked Latrobe to select carriages for the White House. In line with his usual practice of making his purchases in Philadelphia, Latrobe placed an order there with coachmaker Peter Harvie for two carriages. One was to be a handsome chariot for town use, mostly by Dolley, and the other was to be a neat coachee for traveling. The specifications for the chariot included that it be a very beautiful reddish brown, in accord with Mrs. Madison's wishes, with a cloth lining costing eleven dollars a yard. When the chariot arrived in Washington, it was far short of meeting the high standards which both Latrobe and Dolley expected. It was no more durable than a one-horse shay. The coachee was rushed to completion in time for a spring journey to

Montpelier.[4] Because of the inferior quality of this work, a long series of letters evolved between Dolley and Latrobe and are here reproduced. The originals of these letters are now in the New York Public Library.

From Philadelphia, Latrobe wrote to the First Lady on March 20th, 1809:

Enclosed are two kinds of lace which I submit to your choice for your chariot. I think I should prefer the narrowest. It is English lace, the yellow part being worsted, of course the color will stand. I could find no other in town that was at all handsome, as it is now become a rare article.—

Your Coachee will certainly be finished by the 15th of May; the Chariot about a fortnight later. I shall send you a number of colors painted on glass for your choice. A Mr. Stevens, a rich Englishman, is here with an English Chariot made in London _____ July. It is very handsome and shows the latest imported. It has given me many hints.

A month later, on April 21, he wrote:

Your letter of the 19th has just been received. Permit me in the first place to thank you for the excellent political news which concludes it.—The interruption of the friendly intercourse thus restored, has cost you individually many an odd dollar extraordinary. For instance: I could not find in the whole city among the merchants a yard of cloth fit to line your carriage, and have at last been obliged to a Tailor (Mr. Alpin) for the quantity required, at $11 per yard. There was not enough for the traveling carriage, and I have been obliged to have recourse to second cloth of somewhat a darker tint, but of the same character of color. The color of your carriage will be a very beautiful redish brown according to your wish. Your taste in this respect agrees with the fashion. The travelling carriage has its first coat, and with favorable weather there is no doubt of your getting it in time. The Chariot is a very neat thing, the most as I recollect to have seen for a long time. I have chosen today the springs, and call almost every day to keep them agoing. . . .

On 7 May, a Sunday, he wrote from Baltimore:

I am here and expected to have been tomorrow in Washington. It is however necessary, I find that I should see Mr. Finley, who is making the chairs and sofas for your Drawing room in his shop, and therefore I shall try tomorrow and arrive in the city on Tuesday.— Your Chariot is in great forwardness, and will be one of the handsomest things Philadelphia has produced. The Coachee has its last coat of paint on, and the Cypher very elegantly managed. I have attended closely to this business and think you will not be disappointed.

But on July 4, while in Washington, he felt constrained to write:

I am more mortified that I can express at the conduct of the coachmaker, I have had the misfortune to employ in your service, in furnishing to you a carriage, which even before it has been used is discovered to be so extremely gaudy. I am the more iritated and disappointed, as he has in every other instance in which I have imployed or recommended him, done himself so much credit, as to have gained the character of being one of the most honest and faithful workmen in Philadelphia. Mr. Harvie, has built for me five carriages of different sorts for my own use, all of which have done me most excellent service, and were universally admired. My present carriage has undergone every possible hardship for three years, and so well is it built, that the first wheels have now their third tire. And still as in your particular case, he so entirely forgotten what is due to you and to his own interest and reputation as regards the coachee, I cannot help thinking that it would be just to throw the chariot upon his hands, especially as there is ample time to get another built before winter. I am sufficiently punished for my own indiscreet zeal by the mortification I suffer and would much rather have been matched in the whole price of the carriage than have occasioned you so much vexation and disappointment. I shall by the mail of this evening write to Mr. Harvie what is proper on the subject, and if you will please to order the deficiencies to be made good, I have the means of throwing the expense of the repair upon his hands— Some small articles are usually required to be altered or amended in every new carriage after the first trial, but no hurry in which this has been built, (it being not yet quite three months since it was ordered) not even the very unfavorable weather for painting it, which has continued nearly the whole of that time can be an excuse for so total a neglect as he seems to have been guilty of, in your opinion.

I hope you will have the goodness to believe that want of judgement on my part, not of the most anxious desire to procure for you a good carriage has led me into the mortifying predicament in which I am.

As to the price (which Mr. Cutts informs me is also thought extravegant) I beg to assure you, that it is below that, which has been given for inferior carriages to Fielding and other fashionable builders by, many of my acquaintance whom I could name.

*With the sincerest respect I am
Madam your obedient humble
Servent*

B. H. Latrobe

P.S. *If you can spare half an hour tomorrow, to ascertain the deficiencies, I will exert myself to have them repaired before you go.*

The carriages proved to be so disappointing that one was returned and its contract cancelled. [5] This was not a fatal blow to Latrobe but it did shake Mrs. Madison's faith in her architect. Her faith was later restored, however, as indicated in a letter she wrote to Latrobe on September 12, 1809, saying "Thirdly, I never for a moment doubted your taste or honour in the direction of public buildings, or even in the building of our little carriage." The little carriage referred to here was of course the coachee. [6]

Whether or not Dolley Madison's carriage was at first satisfactory, she nevertheless must have had a very elegant coach, which is reported to have cost $1,500.[7] The coach seemed to have made a most appropriate vehicle for the First Lady who blossomed out in rich clothes and went royally about the city in her coach and four. Race Week, in November, was one of the highlights of the Washington season and Dolley was there in all her finery. When she evacuated the White House in 1814 just before it was set afire by British soldiers, she gathered the Cabinet papers together into trunks, which were piled into her carriage before she clambered in. The coach, heavily laden with its priceless wares, raced off toward Georgetown and safety. Thus the carriage served many good purposes during Dolley's stay in the White House. When she returned after the fire, she and the President occupied the Taylor House until the Executive Mansion could be rebuilt. No Madison carriages are known to have survived the ravages of time, and, at this late date, the chances are slight that any have survived. Indeed, the author has been unable to locate even pictorial evidence of any of their carriages.

[1] Brant, *James Madison,* Vol. 1, p. 152.
[2] Singleton, *The Story of the White House,* Vol. 1, p. 57.
[3] Undated letter from B.H. Latrobe to Mrs. Madison (Cornell University Library).
[4] Brant, *James Madison, The President 1809-1812,* p. 32.
[5] Hamlin, *Benjamin Henry Latrobe,* p. 302.
[6] *Ibid.,* pp. 328-329.
[7] Hurd, *The White House,* p. 50.

Pleasure wagon used by President James Monroe.

Courtesy of the Shelburne Museum, Inc.

Chapter Five

Rode to his inauguration in
a plain and unostentatious carriage.

James Monroe

AT THE TIME JAMES MONROE assumed office in 1817, the rebuilt White House still had fresh plaster and paint which rendered it damp and disagreeable. More comfortable conditions prevailed at his Oak Hill estate and for some time the family remained there before moving into the White House. The President rode on horseback to Washington on Monday mornings some thirty-three miles and returned to Oak Hill on Saturday.[1]

In a letter to President Monroe, dated July 28, 1818, Mr. James Yard of Philadelphia wrote: "I can procure you a very handsome coachee for $700. It will be a handsome and very useful carriage."[2] Whether Monroe ever purchased this carriage remains unknown.

James Monroe rode to his second inauguration in 1821 in a plain carriage drawn by four horses and manned by a single Negro footman.[3]

With the exception of the hubs of one carriage, nothing remains from any known vehicle used by the fifth President. Occasionally other carriages have turned up which have connections with his family, but they are either too late in date or otherwise unlikely to have been used by him personally.

Perhaps the most interesting of the vehicles associated with James Monroe is a "pleasure wagon," now on exhibit at the Shelburne Museum, Inc., Shelburne, Vermont. This vehicle transported President Monroe during his tour of the Northern states in July of 1817. It was bought in 1888 from a Mr. Kellogg for $45 and presented to the Sheldon Museum, which has loaned it to the Shelburne Museum. The wagon is green; its red wheels are picked out with

43

black. The body displays a light-green acorn stencilled pattern. It is of hand construction and follows the principles of early framing, with mortised and pegged parts, and is one of the oldest carriages in the Shelburne Museum collection. The wagon was licensed in Vergennes, Vermont, by Beldon Seymour.

The inventory of the estate of James Monroe taken at Oak Hill, Virginia, on January 22, 1836, lists one old carriage with an estimated value of $10.[4] There is no indication of who acquired this carriage, but possibly it is the one from which the hubs—now in the possession of his descendant, Laurence G. Hoes, of Fredericksburg, Va.—were later taken.

[1] Upton, *Our Early Presidents,* p. 262.
[2] James Monroe Papers, Series 1, accession 4775, Library of Congress.
[3] Nevans, *The Diary of John Quincy Adams,* p. 260.
[4] Cresson, *James Monroe,* p. 354.
[5] Will Book Y, p. 327, Loudoun County, Virginia.

Chapter Six

His horses ran away with his carriage.
Although he had previously
alighted from the carriage, his coachman
was killed in the accident.

John Quincy Adams

WHEN PRESIDENT-ELECT ADAMS came to the Capitol in 1825 to be inaugurated as the sixth President of the United States, he rode in an open carriage drawn by four bays of fine appearance. He was accompanied by Samuel L. Southard, Secretary of the Navy, and William Wirt, Attorney-General.

There are few records of the White House equipage during the administration of the second President Adams. His diary tells that he had a carriage and four horses and that son John had a gig and a thill horse.[1] In 1825 one of his horses died as the result of a fall while ascending the hill called the Bull's Neck. The President also had a pony which threw him on May 23, 1828, and slightly injured his neck.

It is likely that the carriage he used at the White House was one he had bought while in Europe in 1815 negotiating the peace treaty with England, and later had shipped to this country. An account written in 1870 describes this carriage:

> After being used by him (John Quincy Adams) for many years, it was brought West, and finally landed in the Bruce shop, where it was torn up, and the running gears put under a furniture car. This Adams carriage was a Landau of the present day, opening in the centre, throwing down both ways, and was a great thing, and when built was considered something perfectly wonderful even for London to turn out. It weighed about three thousand pounds, and was drawn by four horses. It was looked upon as such a splendid concern that on the inside, under the lining, was a nice plate with the names of the workmen who had been employed upon it.[2]

When his term of office as President ended in 1829, Adams remained in Washington to serve a long and distinguished term in Congress. Diary entries shed a little light on his riding habits. In 1840, he writes of a coachman named Thomas.[3] The following year he wrote on February 18:

> *There was an exhibition at a quarter past eleven, in the front yard of the Capitol, of firing with Colt's repeating firearm—a new-invented instrument of destruction, for discharging twelve times a musket in as many seconds. I rode to the Capitol with Mr. Smith. We had alighted from the carriage from five to ten minutes, when the firing commenced. My carriage was then going out of the yard; the horses took fright, the carriage was jammed against a messenger's wagon, overset, the pole and whippletree broken, the harness nearly demolished; the coachman, Jeremy Leary, and the footman, John Causten, precipitated from the box, and Jerry nearly killed on the spot. He was taken into one of the lower rooms of the Capitol, where, as soon as I heard of the disaster, I found him, in excruciating torture.*

And the next day:

> *I walked home; and about half-past six, Jeremy Leary died, almost without a groan.*[4]

In the last will and testament of John Q. Adams, dated January 18, 1847, Norfolk County, Massachusetts, the following dispensation was made of his vehicles: "I give to her (his widow) also all my carriages and horses, china, plate, and plated wares as well at Quincy as at Washington."[5]

---

[1] Nevans, *Diary of John Quincy Adams,* pp. 351, 359, 374.
[2] *Coach-Makers' International Journal,* Vol. VI, No. 4, p. 61, which is a portion of an article in the *Cincinnati Weekly News,* Nov. 12, 1870. B. Bruce and Co. was operating in Cincinnati, Ohio, as early as 1828. The Messrs. B. Bruce & Co. included Benjamin Bruce, Isaac and David. After David died in 1837 the business was run by the other two. Isaac later went south. In 1863, Isaac retired leaving the business as B. Bruce & Co.
[3] Nevans, *Diary of John Quincy Adams,* p. 507.
[4] *Ibid.,* p. 517.
[5] Fielding, *The Wills of the Presidents,* p. 73.

Chapter Seven

"President Jackson used to visit his stable every morning, until he became feeble, and he paid special attention to the manner in which his horses were shod."

Andrew Jackson

THERE ARE SEVERAL accounts of Andrew Jackson's coming to Washington for his first inauguration in 1829. One tells of how he left a riverboat at Wheeling, West Virginia, where a Mr. James Reeside offered him a fine new coach worth $500. It had his name painted in bright colors on its sides, but he declined it because of his custom of refusing gifts. Since on a later occasion, however, he did accept a fine coach as a gift, it is difficult to understand why he refused the Reeside offer.[1] Tradition relates that he turned down the offer and rode in another coach, but that he arranged for the Donelsons to ride in this one.

A second account of this trip is recorded by Bryan, who reports that Jackson drove to Washington nearly three weeks prior to his inauguration in the carriage of the Senator from Tennessee, John H. Eaton.[2] Another account states that the Whigs of Baltimore presented to the President-elect a coach to be used in the inauguration, but Jackson did not accept that one either.[3]

On the day of the inauguration Jackson walked down the street accompanied by a bodyguard. After the ceremonies he mounted his white charger and, with great difficulty, made his way down Pennsylvania Avenue surrounded by a dense mob all the way to the White House, which had been vacated the day before by John Quincy Adams.[4] At his second inaugural in 1833, Jackson took the oath of office in the House of Representatives and thus avoided ceremonies.

During Jackson's second term in office, the old frame stable at the end of the east wing of the White House was removed, and a hundred yards to the east a new stable was built to accommodate ten horses.[5]

The carriage used by Jackson at the White House for state, ceremonial, and social purposes, and in which he made several trips to The Hermitage, his beloved Tennessee home, was of a Philadelphia make. The builders sent two from which to choose. One was lined with blue uncut velvet, while the other had red. Both Jackson and his daughter-in-law, Sarah, chose the red. The gaily-lined carriage was drawn by six white horses.[6]

Jackson's carriage was exhibited at one time in the Tennessee Centennial Exhibition in Nashville. The President's nephew and adopted son, Colonel Andrew Jackson, sold the carriage to the Ladies' Hermitage Association. It is now on exhibit in the carriage house of The Hermitage, its brilliant lining faded to a light rose.

When Jackson's second term was ended, he spent two weeks in the White House as the guest of his successor, resting before the long journey home,[7] which he made in this carriage. It was well that he rested, for the trip took thirty days. Jackson and his daughter-in-law occupied the back seat of the coach and Dr. Gwynn, his personal physician, sat in front. The grandchildren rode along in a chartered stagecoach (which overturned on the way back). Along the journey, Jackson doled out 150 silver half-dollars to mothers who presented their children. At one point, a wreath of laurel was placed upon the General's head. The wreath was later stowed away in the top of the carriage where it remained for many years.[8] A letter about the purchase of this carriage by Mrs. Rachel Jackson Lawrence is today on exhibit with the vehicle.

In Anne Wharton's *Social Life in the Early Republic* one finds mention of the carriages being prepared for Jackson:

> *A superb coach and eight white horses is ready in Philadelphia. A carriage built of hickory is getting ready in Baltimore, and a vessel called the "Constitution" is to be borne here full sail by sixteen white horses.*
>
> *The coach built in Philadelphia, drawn by eight white horses; the hickory carriage, Baltimore's votive offering to Andrew Jackson; and another conveyance modeled after the "Constitution," did not it seems occupy prominent places in the inaugural ceremonies of March 4, 1829, as, according to Mrs. Harrison Smith, General Jackson, after taking the oath of office, mounted his horse and rode home from the Capitol, having gone thither on foot.*[9]

Whether Jackson received the carriage from Philadelphia or Baltimore is not clear, but N. P. Willis, the American poet, was visiting Jackson at the White

House and described a sulky made of hickory, presumably the one presented to Jackson by the Whigs of Baltimore. Says Mr. Willis:

> Some eccentrik mechanick has presented President Jackson with a sulky made of rough cut hickory, with the bark on. It has very much the everlasting look of "Old Hickory" himself, and if he could be seen driving a high-stepping, bony old iron-gray steed in it, any passer-by would see that there was as much fitness in the whole thing as in the chariot of Bacchus and his reeling leopards. Some curiously-twisted and gnarled branches have been very ingeniously turned into handles and whip-box, and the vehicle is compact and strong. [10]

On January 8, 1837, a group of sixty Democratic-Republican friends presented President Jackson with an elegant carriage made from timbers of the old ship *Constitution*. Accompanying the carriage was the following letter, the original of which is in The Hermitage at Nashville:

> "New York January 8th 1837
> to ANDREW JACKSON, President of the United States;
> SIR;
>
> A number of your Democratic Republican fellow citizens, residents of this city, being desirous to express their estimation of your character and public service, on occasion of your retirement from the high office which you have filled for the last eight years with so much credit to yourself, and with such signal advantage to our common country, and also to manifest to you their earnest and sincere conviction, that during your administration, you have conducted its affairs with the noble view of restoring the government to pure constitutional principals, and with unceasing care and an unerring eye to the public good beg (through us, a committee appointed for that purpose) your acceptance of the   PHAETON herewith presented.
>
> The committee are sensible that their present possesses no other value, than that of having been made out of the timber which originally formed part of the United States frigate CONSTITUTION a ship which more than any other in our Navy, has contributed by her gallant victories in the late war, to impart lustre to the American name and character and it appeared fiting that this remnant of the noble ship which had so often borne in triumph the flag of our country should be appropriated to the service of the distinguished individual, who in war gloriously asserted and in peace has firmly maintained and defended the rights of the nation to which she belonged.
>
> On behalf of our Constituants as well as ourselves we tender you the assurance of our high respect for your person and of gratitude for your services.
>
> Your friends and fellow citizens

This elegant phaeton was made at Amherst, Massachusetts, of fine-grained oak timbers from the frigate *Constitution*. The unpainted wood had been varnished until it shone. It contained a seat for two and a driver's box covered with superb hammercloth, set up rather high in front. The wheels and body

Original panel showing "Old Ironsides" in full sail.
Courtesy of Ladies' Heritage Association

Courtesy of the Ladies' Hermitage Association

Phaeton made of wood from "Old Ironsides" and presented to President Andrew Jackson.

Andrew Jackson enroute to the capital for his inauguration in 1829.

Courtesy of the Ladies' Hermitage Association

Coach used by President Andrew Jackson at the White House for state, ceremonial and social purposes and for several trips to the Hermitage.

were low, with bars behind for baggage. The wheels were very slender and light, but strong and capable of a great deal of service. On the door panels on either side was a picture of "Old Ironsides" under full sail. Jackson's four iron-gray carriage horses, with brass-mounted harness, drew the phaeton when it was used by Martin Van Buren on March 4, 1837, the day of his inauguration. General Jackson, against the advice of his physician, had risen from his sickbed to ride with his successor. Cheers went up from the crowds as they rode together down newly-paved Pennsylvania Avenue, the first President and President-elect to ride in the same carriage.[11]

President Van Buren later sent the phaeton to General Jackson shortly after Jackson returned to Tennessee. In an accompanying letter Van Buren wrote: "My dear friend, I have sent you by the same vessel that conveys to you the Constitutional carriage a quarter cask of old and excellent sherry."[12] Jackson used this carriage during his last years, because it was low and easy to step into. The phaeton was later burned in a fire in Cincinnati, where Colonel Jackson (son of the General's adopted son) was then living and had his family mementos stored. The burned skeleton of the phaeton is today exhibited at The Hermitage together with the letter from the citizens presenting it to Jackson and a photograph of the phaeton before it was burned.

Jackson named his favorite horse, "Truxton," after Commodore Thomas Truxton, the commander of the U.S.S. *Constitution*.[13]

---

[1] *American Motorist*, Mar. 1933, p. 6.
Searight, *The Old Pike*, p. 176.
[2] Bryan, *History of the National Capital*, Vol. 2, p. 213.
[3] Unidentified newspaper clipping, Library of the Architect of the Capital.
[4] Leupp, *Walks About Washington*, pp. 157-158.
Bryan, *History of the National Capital*, Vol. 2, p. 213.
Hurja, *History of Presidential Inauguration*, p. 26.
[5] *Intelligencer*, Nov. 18, 1834.
[6] Upton, *Our Early Presidents*, p. 377.
[7] Smith, *Peculiarities of the Presidents*, p. 103.
[8] Willets, *Inside History of the White House*, p. 437.
[9] Wharton, *Social Life In the Early Republic*, pp. 232, 236.
[10] Singleton, *The Story of the White House*, Vol. 1, pp. 219, 232.
Willets, *Inside History of the White House*, p. 103.
[11] Jeffries, *In and Out of the White House*, p. 103.
Evening Star, Jan. 16, 1937.
Harper's Weekly, Mar. 14, 1857, p. 169.
Hurja, *History of Presidential Inaugurations*, pp. 28, 29.
Washington Post, Jan. 20, 1949.
Willets, *Inside History of the White House*, p. 434.
[12] Martin, *After the White House*, p. 143.
[13] Jones, *Homes of the American Presidents*, p. 60.

From the Boston Post, Boston, Massachusetts

Carriage once used by President Martin Van Buren and later owned by a Mr. Samuel J. Shaw of Brookline, Massashusetts.

Chapter Eight

"His olive green Presidential coach, silver mounted harness and liveried men on the box which was a familiar sight on the Washington streets, was considered an evidence of extravagant and luxuriant living by his political opponents."

Martin Van Buren

WHEN MARTIN VAN BUREN was a young man, he acquired a victoria carriage which had been custom-built in England; all its iron work was hand-forged. It had C-springs and was suspended by leather through-braces. There was a coat-of-arms on each of its four panels. Van Buren did most of his campaigning in this carriage and, in 1824 and 1825, when General Lafayette visited the United States, it was in this same vehicle that the two gentlemen rode from Albany, New York, to Washington, D.C.

In 1832, prior to his election to the Presidency, Martin Van Buren brought from England a coach for which he paid $1,550 to use in touring literary and historical shrines.[1]

Some weeks before Van Buren was elected President, his gig was involved in an accident which damaged the vehicle so that it required some repairs. Writing to Van Buren on October 8, 1836, a certain Francis Blair explained that if he were asked anymore about the accident, he would frankly say "that you (Van Buren) were not in the carriage at the time of the accident."[2] Apparently the newspapers were building upon the story, and this was a source of irritation to the presidential candidate.

According to a nineteenth-century account, "Martin Van Buren had a fine turnout while he was in the White House. His carriage was a dark olive hue, with ornaments as bright as burnished gold. He had a footman and coachman in livery, and he rode about in grand style."[3] The harness was silver mounted and the coachmen were attired in green to match the carriage. On Inauguration

55

Day, however, the President-elect chose to ride at the side of President Jackson, in the phaeton which had been shaped from the timbers of the frigate *Constitution* and presented to Jackson near the close of his administration.[4]

Like many of the early Presidents, Martin Van Buren was fond of horseback riding and frequently did so before breakfast. After retiring to New York from the White House he regularly attended the Dutch Reformed Church, riding usually in his coach, but during the winter months he preferred to wrap himself in his buffalo robes and ride in a sleigh.[5]

None of the vehicles used by the eighth President are known to survive. The last one of which evidence exists is the victoria carriage from England.

The victoria was later taken to Auburn, New York, where it was purchased by Mr. Samuel J. Shaw of 1232 Beacon Street, Brookline, Massachusetts. Mr. Shaw had the idea of exhibiting it in the railroad pageant at the World's Fair at New York in 1939.[6] Mr. Shaw died without heirs on February 29, 1944, in his 65th year, and the present whereabouts of the carriage is unknown.

---

[1] Holmes, *The American Talleyrand—The Career and Contemporaries of Martin Van Buren, Eighth President*, p. 281.
Martin, *After the White House*, p. 162.
[2] Martin Van Buren Papers, Library of Congress, Item 5550, letters received.
[3] *The Blacksmith and Wheelwright*, Vol. 16, No. 5, Nov. 1887, p. 369.
[4] *American Motorist*, Mar. 1933, p. 7.
Leeming, *The White House in Picture and Story*, p. 34.
Lorant, *The Presidency*, p. 143.
[5] Martin, *After the White House*, p. 166.
[6] *Boston Post*, May 12, 1939.

Chapter Nine

He rode to the Capitol for his inauguration
on his white charger, caught cold
and died a month later.

William Henry Harrison

As A RESULT OF THE DESTRUCTION of William Henry Harrison's papers by fire in July 1858 at North Bend, there is little recorded today concerning the transportation habits of our ninth President.

In the surviving Harrison records there is mention that Titus W. Vigus of Cincinnati sold to Harrison and Israel L. Ludlow a four-horse covered wagon, a grey six-year-old, and two bays, aged four and ten. This transaction took place sometime prior to December 8, 1828. [1]

The diary of John Quincy Adams records that the President-elect rode down Pennsylvania Avenue the day of his inauguration "on a mean-looking white horse, in the centre of seven others, in a plain frock-coat or surtout, undistinguishable from any of those before, behind or around him." [2] A group of Baltimore Whigs had presented the General with a coach for the occasion but the hero of Tippecanoe preferred to ride on his white charger. [3] A month before the inauguration, a certain Charles McAllaster of Philadelphia had written to the General in Ohio on February 10, 1841, saying:

> Mr. Newrich the Pres. of the Baltimore R.R. Co. has very kindly offered to send your horse to Baltimore free of expenses but he has been obliged to send for a horse car & I will not be able to get him off until Friday morning. [4]

This, presumably, was the white charger which the General rode on March 4th.

When the inventory of President Harrison's property was made on January 1, 1842, [5] there was mention of his coachman John, and the following personal property "appraised at the Point as the property of Gen. Wm. H. Harrison:"

1 colt, 2 yrs old
1 sorel mare (Irwins)
1 old brown horse (now at the Bend) (Bob)
1 old black horse (Mike and since dead)
1 black yearling colt
1 old horse cart $4
2 yoke of oxen
1 bay horse (Charley)
2 ox wagons

The inventory of the personal property at North Bend showed the following:

Old Family carrage $15.00
1 yoke oxen
1 old bay horse (John)
1 brown bay horse (Toby)
1 brown mare
1 sorrel horse
1 cream-colored horse (colt sold Hyatt)
Brown mare and mule colt
1 yearling mule colt
1 2-yr old mule colt
1 ox wagon
1 light wagon
New carriage $500.00

From this we can conclude that the President had at least two carriages at the time of his death, but their whereabouts today remains unknown.

---

[1] William Henry Harrison Papers, Library of Congress (Being papers found years later with the Benjamin Harrison Papers and sent to the Library of Congress.)
[2] Nevins, *Diary of John Quincy Adams*, p. 519.
[3] Hurja, *History of Presidential Inaugurations*, p. 31.
[4] William Harrison Papers, Library of Congress.
[5] *Ibid.*

Chapter Ten

His boat was more elegant than his carriages and was named "Pocahontas."

John Tyler

WHEN THE TYLER FAMILY first moved into the White House, they owned a second-hand carriage. The carriage was purchased at the sale of the effects of Mr. Paulding, the Secretary of the Navy under Mr. Van Buren. The President used the carriage for over a month displaying the Paulding coat-of-arms emblazoned on the door panels. It wasn't until after Mr. Wise of Virginia had criticized him that he ordered the Paulding armorial bearings to be painted over. Along with the carriage, he also purchased some previously worn suits of livery. These he later used for the Negro waiters to wear at state dinners. [1]

Soon the Tylers drove a fine coach complete with liveried coachmen and footmen. In fact, Mrs. Tyler was ridiculed for driving with four horses which were finer than those of the Russian minister. [2] No description survives of the state carriage other than a mention in a letter which Mrs. John Tyler wrote to her mother in 1845: "I am becoming very well contented with my rockaway carriage though it looked mighty insignificant I must confess with my state carriage still in my mind's eye—It seemed as severe as amputation to exchange that and $200 for it." [3]

That the rockaway was an unpretentious vehicle is borne out repeatedly in the many references which Mrs. Tyler makes to "my little carriage." [4] At this time the Tylers had returned from the White House and had retired to their home at Sherwood Forest in Virginia, the reason for buying a smaller carriage.

The rockaway remained for several generations at Sherwood Forest and today the lights from the carriage adorn the doorway to the family home still

59

President Tyler leaving his carriage to board the boat for his return trip to Virginia from the White House.

occupied by a Tyler descendant. Concerning the carriage, the granddaughter, Mary Lyon Tyler (Mrs. George Peterkin Gamble) wrote in 1964:

> *I do not have a picture of it but I remember it well. When I was a child it stood in the stable yard at 'Sherwood Forest,' under a large cedar tree. We used to play in it pretending it was Cinderalla's coach, because it suggested the coaches in the pictures of that era. It had not been used for sometime then because it was in very ill repair and the roads were not smooth enough in Virginia for such a handsome vehicle. Although so very old in my time it was in fairly good condition, a large black coach lined with gray broadcloth and velvet with cushioned seats and the two lanterns on either side of the coachman's seat. The tongue indicated that it took two or four horses and I think there was a step at the back for the footman. Unfortunately it burned up when the stable burned in about 1907, as I remember.* [5]

The description of the carriage is interesting and does coincide with that of a rockaway. Others have also related the same story about the stable burning with the carriage inside. Thus, with the burning of the rockaway and the disposition of the state carriage by the Tylers themselves, there remains today no complete coach with a Tyler association, only the lights from the rockaway.

A much more elaborate description is preserved of Tyler's boat than of any of his carriages. To visit their neighbors while living at Sherwood Forest, "they went in a finely-upholstered oar-pelled boat, the *Pocahontas* which had cushions of drab damask satin trimmed with blue. According to Mrs. Tyler, the four oarsmen wore uniforms of bright blue and white check calico shirts, white linen pants, black patent leather belts, straw hats painted blue, with 'Pocahontas' upon them in white, and in one corner of the shirt collar (which turned down) is worked with braid of bow and arrow (to signify from the Forest) and in the other corner the President's and my initials." [6]

---

[1] Martin, *After the White House*, p. 184. Wharton, *Social Life In The Early Republic*, p. 295.
[2] Tyler Papers, Vol. 8—Item 655, Letter from Mrs. Tyler at Sherwood Forest to her mother dated Oct. 6, 1845.
[3] Tyler Papers, Vol. 8, Letter to her mother dated Sherwood Forest, May 27, 1845.
[4] *Ibid.*, Letter dated White Sulphur Springs, Greenbrier Co., Va., Aug. 16, 1845.
[5] Letter to Herbert R. Collins from Mary Lyon Tyler Gamble, dated Jan. 8, 1964.
[6] Martin, *After the White House*, p. 184.

Chapter Eleven

**Refused the gift of a fine riding horse
sent to the White House stable
and ordered it returned to the owner.**

James K. Polk

PRESIDENT-ELECT POLK rode to his inauguration in an open carriage with the outgoing President. Mr. Polk stood most of the way, greeting the cheering crowd along the avenue.

President Polk brought with him to the White House a very handsome carriage "of dark olive highly polished, and with gilt borders around the panel work. The cushions of the interior were of rich figured cloth, with lace trimmings, and the windows had curtains of blue and red figured stuff. He drove four horses, and his equipage was one of the sights." [1]

Soon after Polk assumed office, an admirer presented him with a fine riding horse. The President declined the offer, sending the horse to the livery stables and sending word to the donor that he could not accept a gift as large as a horse. Another attempt by a group of New York citizens to present him with a carriage and horses was also declined, and that discouraged further offers. [2]

President Polk's fine carriage fell into ruins in the late 19th century and was last exhibited at the Columbian Exposition of 1893. Mary H. Krout, correspondent for the *Chicago Inter-Ocean,* wrote a very strong article on the abuse and care of the object saying: "In a prominent place, against the north wall (of the Transportation Building), is all that remains of President Polk's carriage. It is a melancholy ruin and is exhibited by the Columbus Buggy Company. It is a sad contrast to the trim well-preserved sedan chair that had attained a dignified age years before the Polk carriage was thought of, and it illustrates how little we care for the possessions of those who have held high places, but who have passed from the stage of action and are forgotten. The linings of the old carriage hang in tatters, the wheels and body, and the remains of the hammer-cloth upon the lofty seat in front, are gray with the dust of many decades. The lamps are also crusted with dust." [3]

[1] The *Blacksmith and Wheelwright,* Vol. 16, No. 5, Nov. 1887, p. 369.
[2] Nelson, *Memorials of Sarah Childress Polk,* p. 89.
[3] *Inter-Ocean,* Chicago, Aug. 2, 1893.

Drawing of President James K. Polk's carriage as it appeared in 1893.

From the Inter-Ocean, Chicago, Illinois

Chapter Twelve

Allowed his war horse "Old Whitey" to graze on the White House lawn during his Administration.

Zachary Taylor

AN INTERESTING ACCOUNT of President-elect Taylor's ride over the mountains on his way to Washington to be inaugurated was recorded in Schart's history of western Maryland. It was reprinted in a history of the Old Pike (now U.S. 40) as follows:

> President Taylor and his party were, in 1849, conveyed over the road under the marshalship of the most indefatigable Whig, Thomas Shriver, who, with some other Cumberlanders, proceeded to the Ohio river and met the presidential party. Among the party were statesmen, politicians, and office-hunters, notably Col. Bullet, a brilliant editor from New Orleans, who was to occupy a relation to President Taylor something like that of Henry J. Raymond to Lincoln. The road was a perfect glare of ice, and everything above ground was literally plated with sleeted frost. The scenery was beautiful; to native mountaineers too common to be of much interest, but to a Southerner like Gen. Taylor, who had never seen the like, it was a phenomenon. In going down a spur of Meadow Mountain, the presidential coach, with the others, danced and waltzed on the polished road, first on one side and then on the other, with every sign of an immediate capsize, but the coaches were manned with the most expert of the whole corps of drivers. Shriver was in the rear, and in the greatest trepidation for the safety of the President. He seemed to feel himself responsible for the security of the head of the Nation. Down each hill and mountain his bare head could be seen protruding through the window of his coach to discover if the President's coach was still upon wheels. The iron gray head of the General could almost with the same frequency be seen outside of his window, not to see after anybody's safety, but to look upon what

seemed to him an arctic panorama. After a ride of many miles the last long slope was passed and everything was safe. At twilight the Narrows were reached, two miles west of Cumberland, one of the boldest and most sublime views on the Atlantic slope. Gen. Taylor assumed authority and ordered a halt, and out he got in the storm and snow and looked at the giddy heights on either side of Wills creek, until he had taken in the grandeur of the scenery. He had beheld nothing like it before, even in his campaigns in Northern Mexico. The President-elect was tendered a reception on his arrival at Cumberland, and the next morning he and his party left on the cars for Washington. [1]

Under a snow-spitting sky, President-elect Taylor and President Polk rode to the Inauguration in 1849 in an open carriage drawn by four greys and escorted by a bodyguard of one hundred horsemen. So great were the crowds that the "Old Hero" could hardly make his way from his hotel to the carriage. When the ceremony was over, the new President and the outgoing President re-entered the carriage for the traditional drive down Pennsylvania Avenue to the White House, but Polk rode only as far as the Irving Hotel.

President Taylor's stay in the White House was curtailed by illness following a near-sunstroke he suffered at the dedication ceremony of the Washington Monument. Although the entire equipage of his stables is not known, his favorite horse and war companion "Old Whitey" was pastured on the White House lawn during Taylor's brief administration. A traveler, N. P. Willis, who visited the Nation's Capitol, was so impressed by the animal that he wrote in his travel journal the following:

We felt the smoke of Buena Vista and Resaca de la Palma, of Palo Alto and Monterey, pushing us toward the old cannon-proof charger. He went smelling about the edges of the sidewalk—wondering, probably, at such warm weather and no grass—and we crossed over to have a nearer look at him, with a feeling that the glory was not all taken from his back with the saddle and holsters. "Old Whitey" is a compact, hardy, well-proportioned animal, less of a battle-steed, in appearance, than of the style usually defined by the phrase "family-horse," slightly knock-kneed, and with a tail (I afterwards learned) very much thinned by the numerous applications for "a hair of him for memory." He had evidently been long untouched with a curry-comb—the name of "Old Whitey," indeed, hardly describing with fidelity a coat so matted and yellow. But remembering the beatings of the great heart he had borne upon his back—the anxieties, the energies, the defiances of danger, the iron impulses to danger, it was impossible to look upon him without a throb in the throat.

We saw General Taylor himself, for the first time, the next day—with more thought and reverence of course, than had been awakend by looking upon his horse—but with not half the emotion. The "hero-President" has been more truthfully described than any man we ever read much of before seeing.⁵

During the time Zachary Taylor was President, improvements were made in the White House which also included improvements on the stables. At the time he was President, Taylor owned two carriages, one pair of carriage horses, and two sets of double harness.³

In General Taylor's funeral procession, his favorite mount, Old Whitey, walked close behind the body with the stirrups reversed.

¹ Searight, *The Old Pike,* pp. 175, 176.
² Willets, *Inside History of the White House,* p. 435.
³ Fielding, *The Wills of the Presidents,* p. 111

Courtesy of Smithsonian Institution
Artist's conception of President Zachary Taylor mounted on his famous war horse.

Carriage owned and used by President Millard Fillmore in Buffalo, New York.

Courtesy of the Buffalo and Erie County Historical Society

Chapter Thirteen

**Permitted his wife to receive
the gift of a magnificent carriage complete with
harness and horses from
a group of friends in New York State.
Upon leaving the White House
he sold his wife's carriage and purchased
a silver service with the money.**

Millard Fillmore

W HEN MILLARD FILLMORE assumed the Office of President following the sudden death of President Taylor, it was reported that he and a White House attendant, Edward Moran, went to look at a fine carriage which a gentleman leaving the Capital had for sale. The President refused the carriage on the grounds that it was secondhand, whereupon Mr. Moran remarked, "But you see, your excellency, you're only a second-hand president." [1]

The carriage problem soon was solved when a group of friends from New York State, avoiding any political criticism for giving a large gift to the President himself, presented Mrs. Fillmore with a magnificent carriage complete with harness and horses. [2] The horses were presented by the ladies of Albany at a cost of $1,000, while the carriage itself cost $1500. It is assumed that the harness was priced at only $100 since the overall cost was $2600. The carriage was made by Wood, Tomlinson & Co., 410 Broadway, New York, who also made a carriage for the same group to present to Daniel Webster that same year. The presidential carriage was described by one of the donors in a letter to President Fillmore as a "Clarence coach made expressly for the President." He went on to describe it as follows:

> It is made of the richest materials, and finished in a style that reflects credit on the artizans employed to do the work. The body and running gear are painted dark invisible green, and the door panels are relieved by a very... artistical painting representing the coat of arms of New York, with motto 'Excelsior' nicely defined in a

69

scroll. . . . On each side of the driver's box is a silver lamp, very ornamental and chaste. A spread eagle of solid silver surmounts each of the reflectors, and the plated glass, ground and polished, is fitted in diamond-shape, and thus presents a neat and rich appearance. . . . The whole . . . (interior) . . . will excite universal admiration. The seats, the sides, front and back, are covered with rich blue watered silk, through which a vine or springs of white run, that in a glare of light resembles burnished silver. They are stuffed with curled hair of best quality, in rools and diamonds, that make the easiest and most comfortable lounge that has ever been invented. The lace of the carriage is of the same material with large blue and silver bullions attached to the holders. The top is covered with the same rich material which forms a pleasing contrast with the rich Turkey carpet on the bottom of the carriage. . . . To each of . . . (the ten windows) is attached a spring curtain of beautiful blue silk finished with rich festoons and tassels. The handles and rollers are made of pearl and silver. . . . [3]

A writer for a contemporary magazine described the coach as "one of the most elegant vehicles of the kind ever built in this country."[4]

After the Fillmores left the White House, Mrs. Fillmore's fine carriage was sold and an announcement of the sale was printed in a contemporary periodical:

Sale of Mrs. Fillmore's Carriage: When Mr. Fillmore became President, his friends in New York presented to Mrs. Fillmore a splendid carriage and horses, which were used by him and his family until the expiration of his term, when it became a question what should be done with this elegant establishment. Mr. Fillmore's fortune did not justify him in living in a style suitable to such an establishment nor was it comfortable to his tastes and simple habits as a private citizen that he should do so. The articles too, were of a perishable nature, and must soon disappear, and as he desired to perpetuate the remembrance of so munificent a benefaction, it was concluded to sell the whole and expend the proceeds in the purchase of a set of plate. This was done, and the set, consisting of twelve pieces, was manufactured to order in New York and numbered from one to twelve inclusive. The principal article, a servery, has the following inscription, and is intended to descend as an heir-loom in his family, as a imperishable record of his gratitude.

The carriage and horses generously presented to Mrs. Millard Fillmore by the citizens of New York in 1850, Having been sold in 1858, the proceeds are invested in this set of plate, as a perpetual memento of gratitude to the Donors. The carriage was sold in this city (N.Y.) for $391.[5]

The carriage owned and used by Millard Fillmore in Buffalo, New York is today preserved in the Buffalo and Erie County Historical Society.

[1] Smith, *Peculiarities of the Presidents*, p. 92.
Martin, *After the White House*, p. 206.

[2] Listed as donors were: C. V. Newhall, Jos. R. Taylor, Jonathan W. Allen, Seth Greer, Moses Maynard, Jr., Robert H. McCarty, Robert T. Haws, James B. Taylor, Shepherd Knapp, Thomas Cornley, Silas C. Herring, George Briggs, Ambrose C. Kingsland, Henry E. Davies, Jos. V. Varnum, Jr., Charles H. Marshall, Marshall O. Roberts, D. D. Howard, Edmund Griffin, James S. Thayer, William V. Brady, William Tyson, Harvey Hart, Nicholas Dean, Lebedee Ring, Robert Smith.
[3] Rayback, *Millard Fillmore, Biography of a President*, pp. 291-292.
[4] *Gleason's Pictorial Drawing Room Companion*, May 3, 1851, p. 20
[5] *Harper's Weekly*, June 19, 1858, p. 391.

Carriage presented to Mrs. Millard Fillmore by a group of friends from New York State.

From Gleason's Pictorial, Boston, Massachusetts

From Gleason's Pictorial, Boston, Massachusetts

Representation of the carriage and horses presented to President Pierce by the citizens of Boston.

Chapter Fourteen

Just prior to his inauguration
he received the gift of a carriage and horses
from his Democratic friends in Boston.

Franklin Pierce

SHORTLY BEFORE COMING TO the White House, the Pierces suffered a personal tragedy in the loss of their only child, a boy whose accidental death occurred before their very eyes. Solitude marked their four years in the White House and the President, a noted equestrian, found his greatest relaxation in riding his horse late at night.

Just prior to his inauguration, Franklin Pierce was presented with a carriage and horses by his Democratic friends in Boston. The carriage was manufactured by Jason Clapp & Son, of Pittsfield, Massachusetts. It was in this elegant carriage that the handsome Franklin Pierce rode to his inauguration in 1853. A description of the carriage appeared in a March 5, 1853 newspaper:

> It is designed for an open or close carriage, and admirably adapted for either. Its weight is about 1,300 pounds, and unlike any coach ever before built in this country for a similar object, is composed of materials of American growth and manufacture solely. The timber in it, which is now so handsomely shaped, was taken from the lofty mountain tops which surround Pittsfield; the axles are of the manufacture of the celebrated Pomeroy, and made exclusively from gun iron, which renders their breaking an utter impossibility; they are set in bronze boxes, and are so perfectly case-hardened that the sharpest file cannot produce an impression upon them. The cloth with which it is trimmed is of a light fawn drab, made expressly by the Pontoosuc Company from American wool, and is of the finest texture,—it does not look so showy or luxurious as a French brocatelle, but will be vastly superior in point of durability. It is very beautifully squabbed, and the lace and tufts put on with

exquisite skill. The glass is from the house of Caleb G. Loring & Co., Boston, and not a flaw can be detected upon its crystal surface; a delicate sprig is artistically carved out on each corner of the windows, which produces a very fine effect. The lamps are of very elegant form, rich silver plating, and on either side of them an eagle is superbly chiseled out, surrounded by stars, which, to the beholder, assume the appearance of so many glittering diamonds. The color of the body is a drop lake with a contrast of black, and the paint is so perfectly laid on, the hottest tropical sun could not crack it. In fact, all the appointments are carried out in good keeping, and in every respect, it correctly represents what the committee who had its construction in charge intended it should be, a plain, unostentatious republican carriage. The harnesses are of the finest quality, and were made by F. W. Hannaford, Boston, fully sustaining the reputation of this excellent workman; the silver mountings are from the establishment of Jones, Ball & Co., who have exercised their usual skill and judgment in their finishing. Major John C. Boyd superintended the getting up of a complete set of trappings for the horses, which were purchased at Jordon, a beautiful town situated in the western part of the State of New York, by Col. Peter Dunbar, of Boston, who has been untiring in his exertions to procure them, and has succeeded in obtaining one of the finest pair in the country. Their color is bright bay, perfectly matched, both foaled by the same dam, and their sire is the celebrated Golden Farmer; they have frames of great strength, and, at the same time, are most symmetrically proportioned; are sixteen hands high, weigh 1200 pounds each, seven and eight years old, travel very spiritedly and gracefully together; have a short natural pony gait of eight miles an hour, which they can perform on a journey without the least urging; very docile and manageable, and for beauty of figure and action are unsurpassed. It is very gratifying that this whole business has been so perfectly consummated, and that so elegant a gift has been made to one whose position deserves the respect and confidence thus manifested. If we mistake not, Gen. Pierce is a man who will do justice to the post that a great people have called him to; he seems to share the good wishes of all parties, and very little of sectarian bitterness is evinced in any quarter. The picture which we given of this costly and elegant present, is an accurate one; especially has the artist studied the horses, the 'near' one being a playful, gay creature, prances constantly, and shows much of the life he exhibits in the engraving. [1]

In 1851, some admirers of Franklin Pierce ordered from C. P. Kimbal & Co., Norway, Maine, [2] a two-wheeled chaise, a fashionable vehicle in its time. Also referred to as a "one-horse shay" or a "chariot of state," the vehicle was driven across the country to Concord, New Hampshire and presented to the then General Pierce. A work of painstaking care displaying much ironwork, and beautiful curves and scrolls, the vehicle nevertheless cost only $150.00. It was used by President Pierce at the White House. Many years later it was given to his family physician who remodeled and refitted it with a new leather top. About 1879, a son of the manufacturer bought the old carriage. It was still in the possession of his family as late as 1897.[3]

In the east colonnade close to the White House kitchen garden and greenhouse a carriage house was built during the Pierce Administration. It housed the President's carriage and his black saddle-horse "Union." Presiding over the stable was Henry, the coachman, who made it well known that he was not a liveried servant and that he sometimes wore a blue coat with plain brass buttons. Thomas, a stable boy, saddled the horses.[4]

In his will dated Concord, New Hampshire, January 22, 1868, Franklin Pierce disposed of an elaborate saddle and a carriage and sleigh in the following manner: "To Colo. Thomas J. Whipple—my silver mounted Mexican Saddle. To Charles D. Wirton I give the best carriage and sleigh to be selected by himself which I may own at my decease."[5]

[1] *Gleason's Pictorial,* Boston, March 5, 1853. Vol. IV, No. 10, p.1. *New York Tribune,* August 13, 1853.
[2] C. P. Kimbal had his carriage factory in Norway, Maine in 1848. His son, also named C. P. Kimbal, later owned and operated the carriage factory of Kimbal & Co. in Chicago, Ill. This business later passed to the grandson, C. F. Kimbal.
[3] Willets, *Inside History of the White House,* pp. 431, 432. *The Hub,* Vol. 39, May 1897, p. 89.
[4] Nichols, *Franklin Pierce, Young Hickory of the Granite Hills,* pp. 239, 240, 241, 313.
[5] Fielding, *The Wills of the Presidents,* p. 122.

From The Hub, New York, New York

President Pierce's two-wheeled chaise, built by C. P. Kimball and presented to Franklin Pierce in 1851.

Chapter Fifteen

His carriage harness contained
thirty-six buckles heavily plated with
silver and fifty-six B's.

James Buchanan

AT LEAST TWO carriages used by President James Buchanan are known to have been made by a Philadelphia carriage builder. One, ordered by his niece, Harriet Lane, was built by S. W. Jacobs of Philadelphia, a noted manufacturer who worked almost until the end of the 19th century.[1] This was a magnificent carriage, used officially on most public occasions, and admired as a specimen of high design and taste. It was drawn by a span of handsome horses. The accompanying harness—decorated with thirty-six heavily silver-plated buckles and fifty-six "Bs"—was as magnificent as the carriage itself. Like some of his predecessors, it was Buchanan's policy not to accept gifts, and so the cost was immediately covered by his check for $800.[2]

The Jacobs carriage is today in the Melville Collection of the Suffolk Museum at Stony Brook, Long Island. Except for the hammercloth, which is missing, the carriage is much as it was when President Buchanan used it. A photographic plate of the carriage owned by H. L. Jacobs, a son of the builder, was reproduced in a carriage journal after the turn of the century.[3]

A second carriage used by President Buchanan came into the possession of D. T. Hess of Quarryville, Pennsylvania, after Buchanan's death in 1861. Mr. Hess was a successful carriage manufacturer until his death in 1922. His son, who carried on the business for a few years, repainted the carriage and sold it in the early 1890's,[4] but bought it back around 1905. The subsequent lineage of the carriage is yet to be fully established. It is believed, however, that this

tograph by the Lancaster New Era, Lancaster, Pennsylvania

rriage used by President James Buchanan in Lancaster, Pennsylvania, and made by
orge W. Watson of Philadelphia in 1853.

carriage is the one presently at Wheatland which contains a plate stating that it was built in 1853 by George W. Watson, a Philadelphia coachmaker. The carriage, known more commonly as a road coach, or a Germantown, was purchased at public auction on May 18, 1963, by Henry J. Marshall on behalf of the James Buchanan Foundation for the Preservation of Wheatland.

The auction sale was held at Chesterbrook Farms, Berwyn, formerly the home of A. J. Cassatt. The collection was part of the estate of Mrs. Eleanor Cassatt Laird, who had earlier presented a Buchanan memento to Wheatland.[5] The 83-year-old coachman for the Cassatts said that the coach had been known as "Black Maria" and that it had been sent by Richard McGrann, a well-known local horseman, to a niece of Mrs. Laird, arriving by railroad in 1908.

After the President retired, he returned to Wheatland, his Lancaster estate. When he stepped from his barouche a band played "Home Sweet Home" and Harriet Lane is reported to have burst into tears.[6]

At Wheatland, the former President hired a man named John Giles as a gardener-coachman and paid him a salary of $12.00 a month. John Giles dutifully met guests at the station and drove them to the Wheatland mansion in the square carriage drawn by the master's excellent pair of bays.[7]

---

[1] *The Vehicle Dealer,* Vol. 8, Dec. 1905, p. 230.
[2] Smith, *Peculiarities of the Presidents,* p. 64.
[3] *The Vehicle Dealer,* Vol. 8, Dec. 1905, p. 230.
[4] *Carriage and Wagon Builder and American Vehicle,* Vol. 28, No. 9, Sept. 1915, p. 17.
[5] *New Era,* Lancaster, Penn.
[6] *Country Life In America,* p. 181.
[7] Jones, *Homes of the American Presidents,* p. 109.

Courtesy of the Suffolk Museum, Long Island, N.Y.

President James Buchanan's carriage made by S. W. Jacobs of Philadelphia about 1854.

Chapter Sixteen

During a cold winter night of his Administration, the White House stables burned, destroying his son's ponies.

Abraham Lincoln

ABRAHAM LINCOLN WAS FOND of horses from earliest childhood. When the family left Kentucky, he and his father rode one horse while his sister and mother shared the other. As a boy he also rode a horse to the grist mill. The first record of his having bought a horse was in 1835, when he was 26, but that animal he later lost in payment of a debt. In 1842, he purchased a new set of harness for $2.00 from Robert Irwin's store. While practicing law he used a home-made buggy and a rawboned horse whose description appeared in a Springfield newspaper when the animal strayed from its stable. It was "a large bay horse, star in his forehead, plainly marked with harness; supposed to be eight years old; had been shod all around but is believed to have lost some of his shoes, and trots or paces." [1]

The earliest account of a repair to one of Abraham Lincoln's vehicles was in 1843, when Obed Lewis' carriage shop repaired the tire and floor of Lincoln's buggy for $1.25. The following year he had several other repairs completed on his buggy by the same shop. [2]

On June 22, 1852, Lincoln purchased a new carriage from Obed Lewis, carriage maker, for $260.00 for which he paid cash two days later. He still retained his buggy and from time to time had repairs made to it. On June 25, 1859, the carriage was repainted, new silk curtains added, hooks attached and the top oiled for $19.50. Obed Lewis continued to do his repair work. [3]

On January 12, 1860, Lincoln traded in his old buggy to Obed Lewis for $9.25 credit on his account. [4]

The horse Lincoln had when he left Springfield for Washington in 1861 had been used by him for seven years. Just before he left Springfield, he sold the horse for $75.00. The horse was traded more than once, and was finally purchased by a drayman. When the news of the assassination of the President came four years later, another man went immediately and purchased the horse from the drayman for $75.00. He put him on exhibition, and the first day took in $80.00. Before the horse died, the man is said to have made over $25,000 showing him about the country.[5]

Writing about the White House stable during her husband's administration Mary Todd Lincoln lamented that, "There was so many lovely drives around and we have only three carriages at our command."[6]

The most elegant of these carriages was a barouche made by Wood Brothers of New York, and presented to Lincoln by a group of New York merchants at his first inauguration.[7] It was Brett style, hung on six springs with C springs behind, and handsomely carved with a "boot" under the driver's seat.[8] A newspaper writer commented on its appearance in 1893: "Its style is now so nearly obsolete that it seems almost grotesque, and its former trappings of silk, plush, and leather are faded and time-stained; but interwoven as its history is with a man and an epoch which liberty-loving people will always regard with transcendent interest, this queer old carriage has a value beyond any of its modern rivals, however grand."[9] The carriage, 14 feet long, seven feet wide, and seven feet high, was purchased by a wealthy friend of the martyred President and by him sold to Studebaker Brothers who are the present owners. It was in this carriage that President and Mrs. Lincoln rode to Ford's Theatre in Washington, D.C. on the fateful night of April 14, 1865.

The Wood Brothers carriage has probably been displayed in more exhibitions throughout the country than any other presidential carriage and has covered more miles on exhibition than it ever did during its entire use by President Lincoln. It has been on view at such events as the World's Fair in Chicago in 1893, the Labor Day Parade in South Bend, Indiana, in 1899, and the National Horse Show Association in Madison Square Garden in November, 1908. Illustrations of the carriage have appeared in numerous publications.

A second carriage owned by the Lincolns in the White House was a "Clarence" built by Brewster and Company. Its neat lines harmonized with a light and graceful structure. Mrs. Lincoln chose it on the morning of May 14, 1861, while on a trip to New York with her cousin, Elizabeth Todd Grimsley. The cost of the carriage was $900.00. At Mrs. Lincoln's order, an addition was made to the vehicle of the initial "L" painted on the door panels, in an oval, in light colors. This was the only change made and the carriage was sent to

Courtesy of the Chicago Historical Society, Chicago, Illinois

One of three carriages used by President and Mrs. Lincoln during their residence at the White House.

Courtesy of the Studebaker Museum

Carriage built by Wood Brothers of New York and presented to President Abraham Lincoln by a group of New York merchants on his first inauguration. It was in this carriage that he last rode to Ford's Theatre.

Washington on Wednesday by rail through Baltimore. It arrived in time for use that Saturday. It was a rich, yet modest-looking open barouche or *catache de mode,* which was the prevailing fashion of summer carriages. The mountings were plain silverplated. The lining was a brown silk corded material having the appearance of uncut velvet. The body was painted dark brown, the wheels black and striped broadly with dark brown, edged with canary.[10] The Brewster carriage is now exhibited in the Chicago Historical Society in Chicago, Illinois.

A third carriage of which no description is available was later disassembled and a small fragment may be seen in the collections of the Division of Political History at the Smithsonian Institution, a gift of Mrs. A. W. Cunningham in 1927.

President Lincoln was involved in very few carriage mishaps, but Mary Todd Lincoln would have been a bad insurance risk. In June 1861, her carriage horse stumbled and fell, breaking the pole and throwing the driver from the box. Mrs. Lincoln was uninjured. Another accident occurred on the morning of July 2, 1863, as she was returning to the White House from a visit to the Soldier's Home. The driver's seat came loose, he was thrown out, and the frightened horses ran off with the carriage. That same year she was emotionally shaken by another accident when she was riding with the President and an iron hoop caught under the carriage and pierced the back seat.[11]

One of many tragedies during the Lincoln Administration occurred on a cold Wednesday night of February 10, 1864. The brick stable located between the Executive Mansion and the Treasury Department building burned completely, and all the animals it housed were destroyed in the fire. President Lincoln jumped over a boxwood hedge and threw open the stable doors, but the fire had gone too far.

Among the animals lost in the fire were the President's two brown-colored horses, two bay blooded horses which belonged to his secretary, John Nicolay, and two ponies. One pony was Tad's; the other had belonged to little Willie Lincoln who died in 1862. The President was so affected by the loss of his dead son's pony that he wept in the East Room as he watched the smouldering ashes. Tad did not hear of the disaster until next morning, but then he threw himself at full length upon the floor in an uncontrollable manner and refused to be comforted.

The three carriages and the carriage shed were fortunately saved. A newspaper reported the next day that "The fire was undoubtedly the work of an incendiary. The stables were lighted with gas, the pipes of which were protruded from the walls of the building on either side, in the rear of the horses, and all combustible matter was far removed from the jets, and there was no possibility of its taking fire from that cause. The only other fire in the stable was in the stove, and it was not probable it caught there either, for there was no combustible matter in its immediate vicinity, and besides, the indications are that the fire commenced in the end of the building away from the stove.

"The police were promptly on the spot, and officer Stinchcomb arrested a man by the name of Patterson McGee on suspicion of having set the stable on fire. McGee was formerly a coachman for the President, and was seen at the stable about one hour before the fire was discovered. He was committed to jail for a hearing tomorrow morning at 10 o'clock." [12]

In the same fire, Cooper, the President's hackman, lost between three and four hundred dollars in gold, which had been placed in a trunk in the stable, and all of his clothing except what he had on his back. [13]

One of the saddest events which occurred while the Lincolns occupied the White House was the sudden death of their son, Willie. After the funeral services in the East Room, the President, accompanied by Robert Todd Lincoln and Senators Browning and Trumbull of Illinois, drove to Oak Hill Cemetery in Georgetown, D.C. The carriage in which they rode was drawn by two black horses. [14]

Of Lincoln's three hired carriage hands at the White House, coachman Edward Burke was born in Canada and footman Charles Forbes had recently arrived from Ireland. The other coachman, native-born Patterson McGee, remained until he was dismissed the day before the stables burned. [15]

A carriage which conveyed Abraham Lincoln from the railroad station at Ottawa to the scene of the Lincoln-Douglas debate is now exhibited at the La Salle County Historical Museum, Utica, Illinois.

[1] *The Spokesman & Harness World,* Vol. 52, March 1936, p. 10.
[2] Powell, *Lincoln Day by Day,* Vol. 1, p. 212.
[3] Powell, *Lincoln Day by Day,* Vol. 2.
[4] *Ibid.*
[5] Daniels, *Life of Abraham Lincoln,* p. 220.
[6] Randall, *Mary Lincoln,* p. 245.
[7] *Chicago Tribune,* Sept. 10, 1893. *The Blacksmith and Wheelwright,* June 1900, Vol. 41-42, p. 201. *The Hub news,* Vol. 5, May 15, 1895, p. 78. *Carriage and Waggon Builder and American Vehicle,* Vol. 28, No. 11, Nov. 1915, p. 10. *The Vehicle Dealer,* Mar. 1909, p. 236. *The Spokesman and Harness World,* Vol. 53, May 1936, p. 3.
[8] *The Hub,* Vol. 34, Feb. 1893, p. 470.
[9] *The Hub News,* Vol. 5, May 15, 1895, pp. 78-79.
[10] *Evening Star,* May 18, 1861.
[11] Randall, *Mary Lincoln,* p. 226.
[12] *Washington Star,* Feb. 11, 1864.
Powell, *Lincoln Day by Day,* Vo. 3, p. 239.
Willets, *Inside History of the White House,* p. 225.
Carpenter, *Six Months at the White House,* p. 44.
Randall, *Mary Lincoln,* p. 338.
The Daily Morning Chronicle, Feb. 11, 1864.
[13] *Chronicle,* Feb. 12, 1864, p. 2.
[14] Randall, *Mary Lincoln,* p. 285.
[15] Willets, *Inside History of the White House,* p. 179. Pendel, *Thirty-Six Years in The White House,* p. 32.

President Andrew Johnson shown riding in his carriage during a reception parade to the Continental Hotel at Philadelphia in 1866.

Chapter Seventeen

Refused the gift of horses and harness from a group of New York bankers and merchants.

Andrew Johnson

THE EARLIEST RECORD of a vehicle owned by the Johnsons was a two-wheeled cart drawn by a blind pony, which transported him and his mother to Greeneville, Tennessee in September, 1826. [1]

When Andrew Johnson moved into the White House in June 1865 following Mrs. Lincoln's long-delayed departure, Robert Todd Lincoln offered to sell him the Lincoln equipages. President Johnson refused the offer, apparently because he had his own equipage, although no specific mention of it has been found.

The President's family did not arrive at the White House until August, 1865 when two carriages arrived from Greeneville. There were now twelve members of the Johnson family at the White House, including Eliza, her second daughter Mrs. Stover, and Mrs. Stover's children. [2]

Earlier in the summer of 1865, a group of New York bankers and merchants opened a subscription to buy the President a new carriage complete with a span of horses and harness, as had been done several times before by New York entrepreneurs when a new President entered office. The carriage, horses, and harness cost $6,000. President Johnson refused the gift on May 22, 1865 because he had a suspicion that there was something behind it all; besides, he was of the firm policy that the President should not accept large gifts. Concerning the refusal the *Daily National Intelligencer* presented the following account:

The President Declines the Projected Present. New York, May 24. President Johnson has respectfully declined the coach and span of horses tendered him by merchants of this city, for the reason that he has ever held that those occupying high official positions should not accept such presents. He asks, however, that he may be permitted to retain the parchment conveying the sentiments of the donors, regarding it as a mark of high respect from kind friends and loyal citizens. [3]

After the gift had been courteously rejected by the President, it was placed at auction; it sold for about half of its original cost. President Johnson's action brought favorable comments from around the nation. Senator James Dixon wrote from Hartford:

Nothing has ever given more satisfaction to all patriotic & thinking men, than your refusal to accept the present lately offered you by parties in New York. While the purity of the motives of the donors is not doubted, there is something in your declination which appeals to every honest heart—and seems to restore to us the sentiment of our ancient purity. Allow me to say, also, that the eminently graceful & appropriate terms, in which your refusal of the gift was expressed, was most admirable, and gratified your friends only less than the act itself.

Permit me to express the hope that you will spare yourself excessive labor if possible. The hot weather is approaching—and you owe it to the people not to over work. [4]

A similar letter is also found in the Johnson correspondence from a Mr. Legrand Marvin in which he states:

Your response of 22 inst in declining (on principle) Mess Low & others' proffer of a coach, etc. appears in today's "Buffalo Morning Express" & elevates the U.S. as a nation on the standard of purety, dignity & self reliance. I could do no less than bespeak to thee, my grateful emotion for an act, so consonant with the teachings, & practice of this writer, since in 1828, he (a college alumni—a then minor) became principal of an Academy. Presents, & the love of them, tantamount, too often, to adulturation, & flattery, if not bribery, were practised, & craved by unpatriotic presidents,—the weakness of even the stern Jackson. Thanks to Providence, for this, your practicality fit successor, to the many pure undying utterances of Abraham Lincoln. May citizens & officers, Civil & Military, learn the lesson—that "consciousness of doing one's "duty," is the purest, most solacing of gratifications & thereby, became purely, & practically "men." Thus in 1832, responded this writer to unsought proffers to him, of office (to be at his selection) in the then dominant party, of course, under an implied "Van Burentic" quid pro quo; alias "barter of conscience," to act, not "pro bono publico," but "qui vive vanditti," (in plain English robber phrase—"to the victors belong the spoils," thereby constituting one's Country—the "body politic" the no longer fabled, but real "honey-ed carcass." May we hope that soon the Sun of Patriotism, Man's best weal-true

> "demo-cracy," (people's rule) the practically right, without show, fuss, or feathers will thrill & genial-ize every office bearer, till all become of cordial esteem for thee, as a firm-practical friend of right doing. [5]

President Johnson hired a tall French Canadian named Nicolas to tend his horses. Nicolas had a habit of going out early in the morning to conduct tourists around the capital in the President's carriage. When the President discovered this, he immediately dismissed Nicolas from his staff. [6]

President Johnson was visiting his daughter, Mrs. Stover, when he died in 1875. The last carriage ride he took was from the depot to the Stover residence. The carriage—no longer in existence but remembered by Johnson descendants—was made by John Brown and Sons of Morristown, Tennessee. A photograph which dimly shows the carriage in front of the residence is still preserved by members of the Stover family.

---

[1] *Messages and Papers of the Presidents,* Vol. 6, 1861-1869, p. 301.
[2] Milton, *The Age of Hate,* p. 229.
[3] *Daily National Intelligencer,* Washington, D.C., Thurs., May 25, 1864, p. 3.
[4] Andrew Johnson papers, L.C. Letters Received, Hartford, Conn., May 26, 1865.
[5] Andrew Johnson papers, L.C. Letters Received, Buffalo, N.Y., May 26, 1865.
[6] Pendel, *Thirty-Six Years in The White House,* p. 53.

General Grant's Arabian stallion, "The Panther."

Courtesy of Library of Congress

Carriage built by Wood Brothers, New York, and used by President U. S. Grant during his second administration.

Courtesy of Smithsonian Institution

88

Chapter Eighteen

Was arrested in Washington for speeding, paid his $20.00 fine and complimented the policeman for doing a good job.

Ulysses S. Grant

NO PRESIDENT WAS FONDER of fine horses than U. S. Grant. In his class at West Point he earned the highest mark for horsemanship and he excelled in high jumping. His love for fast horses brought him the distinction of being the only President arrested during his term of office. A Negro policeman arrested him for exceeding the speed limit while driving his spirited team through the Washington streets. The President politely paid his $20.00 fine on the spot and commended the policeman for excellent execution of his duty.

Senator John P. Jones related the following incident which took place on the White House grounds:

> *A butcher in Washington owned one of the finest driving horses I ever saw, and from the moment Grant clapped his eyes on the proud, high-stepping animal his very soul yearned to possess it. He dared not tell anybody of his desire to own the horse because he feared some overzealous friend or scheming lobbyist would buy it and give it to him. Only to me did he confide this secret of his heart—for such it really was.*
>
> *I watched developments with keen interest, confident what the outcome would be in spite of my knowledge that Grant was never harder up than he was just then. Congress had not at that time increased the President's salary from twenty-five thousand dollars, and Grant actually needed every cent of his salary to make both ends meet. But just as I confidently expected, it wasn't long before Grant bought the butcher's horse. He had to give six hundred dollars for it. The day after the purchase Grant invited Conkling and me to see the horse, though just why he wanted Conkling—who cared nothing*

at all for horses—to come along I was unable to guess, unless it was that he wanted to get another lecture from the imperious New Yorker for extravagance.

Isn't he fine, Jones? Grant said to me.

I assented.

Don't you think he's magnificent, Conkling? Grant then exclaimed, stroking the animal's fine mane.

I guess he'll do, replied Conkling. But how much did you give for him.

Six hundred dollars, responded Grant.

Umph! snapped Conkling. All I have got to say is that I would rather have six hundred dollars than the horse.

That's what the butcher thought, said Grant, and he nudged me in the ribs with an elbow. [1]

A second version of how President Grant acquired this horse, which he subsequently named "Butcher's Boy," contradicts the first story. This account tells that President Grant was riding down the street in a light rig and saw the horse hitched to a butcher's wagon. When the two vehicles were even in the street, they began a lively race in which the wagon, driven by the butcher's boy, won. Shortly thereafter the President sent one of his friends to look at the horse and purchase it for him.[2] Regardless of which account is accurate, the horse did wind up in the White House stable. Here his companions were "Cincinnatus," a dark bay charger; "St. Louis" and "Egypt," matched carriage horses; "Julia," for the buggy; "Billy Button" and "Reb," the Grant boy's Shetland ponies; "Jeff Davis," a saddle horse quite hard to manage; and "Algonquin," the boy's calico pony; "Jennie" and "Mary," the property of Miss Nellie Grant; and three Hambletonian Colts.[3] "Cincinnatus" was the President's favorite saddle horse because he was never frightened by the commotion in the capital's streets and could be left unhitched and unattended for long periods of time. The President's day was not complete until he had visited the stables, giving each of the inhabitants a kind word and pat. "Cincinnatus" and "Egypt" were the pride of the President's stable.

"Reb" and "Billy Button" pulled the school cart for the President's children each day. "Reb" had been captured in the Vicksburg campaign and presented to Frederick Grant, the President's oldest son. "Billy Button" belonged to the era of peace.

During President Grant's Administration new White House stables were built. Once during his administration three of the horses strayed from the stables and it cost the President $6.00 to redeem them.

In addition to choosing fine horses and ponies for each member of his family, Grant considered their tastes and wishes in planning the equipages.

The White House fleet consisted of a landau, barouche, top buggy, pony phaeton, and road wagon. At least two Negro coachmen, Charlie Lee and Albert Hawkins, formed the stable staff. On one occasion when Hawkins was late arriving with the buggy, the President paced the White House portico in army style and smoked his cigar, patiently waiting for the coachman, who was inexcusably late. When he finally did arrive, the President greeted him with a few kind words, took the reins and went about his way.

One of the earliest vehicles used by Ulysses S. Grant was a two-horse carriage he bought while living in Georgetown Heights in the summer of 1865. He used the carriage until after he became President. Early in the summer of 1870 President Grant ordered a new carriage, and he gave the old one to Daniel Ammen, Rear Admiral, U.S.N. (Retired). Concerning the carriage Mr. Ammen later wrote:

> *I herewith give an authentic account of the two horse carriage given me by General Grant in the early part of the summer of 1870. He bought the carriage when living on Georgetown heights, soon after coming to Washington, in the summer of 1865, and had no other carriage until after he became the occupant of the White House. There is no mark of the maker's name on it. No further conversation that I can recall, occurred between the General and myself, relating to this, than his saying he had a very good carriage for the country and would send it out to me if I would accept it. I thanked him, and said it would be very acceptable, and the carriage was sent to me in a few days.*
>
> *To avoid error in my statement, I called on Mr. Richard Curtin, who for very nearly ten years was in the employ of the General. He has entire recollection and informs me of the fact that the General had no other carriage in Washington before he resided in the White House. He remarked on the build of the carriage, with a coupling pole, and said that about the time the General gave me the carriage the use of a coupling pole was abandoned.*

In 1888, Admiral Ammen deposited the carriage in the United States National Museum with the understanding that it was to be returned to his son, Ulysses Grant Ammen, after July 4, 1900. The carriage was returned to the family as requested in 1906 and was sold at public auction in Washington, D.C., on November 23, 1906 for the sum of $3.00. The purchaser is unknown.[4]

In 1870, the President purchased a new carriage from Wood Brothers, New York, New York, and Bridgeport, Connecticut. The carriage cost $1,200 and weighed about 1,000 pounds.[5] The carriage is described thus:

> *It presented interesting features as to excessive height and general design. The body was raised above the axles on exceedingly high springs, which elevated the seat of the occupants, who were carried at a height considerably above the passengers of other vehicles used*

Courtesy of the Studebaker Museum

Carriage used by President Grant in Washington and later in New York.

From Harper's Weekly, New York, New York

"Reb" and "Billy Button" carrying the President's children to school during the Grant Administration.

in the streets. President Grant frequently made use of this carriage in riding out with Mrs. Grant and in taking his sons out for an airing. The vehicle provided room for four persons, although two more could be crowded in. It was sold shortly after the death of General Grant, and is still in existence (1915), the property of an American carriage builder. The carriage was regarded as a fine specimen of the specially designed custom-made vehicle in its day and generation. [6]

The carriage was originally designed as a sporting carriage, and hunting dogs were carried under the seats. It was in this carriage that President Grant rode in 1873 to attend his second inauguration. Years later the vehicle was purchased by the Samuel J. Meeks Company, Washington, D.C. This carriage was displayed in the George Washington bi-centennial celebration in 1932. [7] In March, 1961, it was loaned to the Committee for the Re-enactment of Lincoln's Inauguration. It was donated to the Smithsonian Institution in 1968 by Fearson S. Meeks.

The landau used by President Grant in Washington, D.C. and in New York after his term of office is presently located in the Studebaker Museum. This carriage was presented to the museum by General Frederick Dent Grant, son of the President, in 1918. [8]

In the Stephen Decatur House in Washington, D.C. hang two paintings of Arabian stallions. The two stallions, "Linden Tree" and "Leopard," were considered rare specimens from the private stables of the Sultan of Turkey. The Sultan presented these stallions to General Grant in 1878 after Grant's world tour. [9]

---

[1] Willets, *Inside History of the White House,* pp. 432, 433.
[2] Colman, *White House Gossip,* pp. 61, 62.
[3] *Perley's Reminiscences on Sixty Years in the National Metropolis,* pp. 258, 259.
[4] U.S. National Museum Accession Papers 22087, dated June 5, 1889.
[5] *The Vehicle Dealer,* Vol. 1, June 15, 1902, p. 266.
[6] *Carriage and Waggon Builder and American Vehicle,* May 1915, Vol. 28, No. 5, pp. 7, 8.
[7] Samuel J. Meeks died October 2, 1899 in his 59th year. His death notice appears in *The Hub,* Vol. 41, Dec. 1899, p. 409. The Company passed into the hands of Meeks's son and was operated in the name of "S. J. Meek's Son." It is presently operated under the same name by grandson, Fearson S. Meeks.
[8] *The Spokesman and Harness World,* Vol. 48, August 1932, p. 23.
[9] *Carriage Dealer's Journal,* May 1915, p. 581. *The Spokesman,* Vol. 31, May 1915, p. 200. *Carriage and Waggon Builder and American Vehicle,* Vol. 28, No. 11, Nov. 1915, p. 17.
[10] Beale, *Decatur House and Its Inhabitants,* pp. 67, 68.

Courtesy of the Rutherford B. Hayes Library

Carriage used by President Rutherford B. Hayes and later by President Garfield. Built by Brewster & Co., New York.

Chapter Nineteen

Was considerate enough to
leave his carriage at the White House
for his successor to use.

Rutherford B. Hayes

DUE TO THE UNCERTAINTY concerning the outcome of the disputed election of 1876, there was no parade or public reception accompanying President Hayes' inauguration on March 5, 1877.

Little is known of the riding habits of President Hayes and his First Lady while they occupied the White House, but their son, Webb Hayes, at the age of 20 learned to ride a bicycle in the East Room of the White House.

When President Hayes entered the White House, he bought a carriage from Brewster and Company of New York at a cost of $1,150. The carriage, known as a barouche, was left at the White House for the use of his successor. In a letter to General Garfield on January 28, 1881, President Hayes said: "In any event my carriage and horses may remain with you as long as you wish. I would not be in a hurry on that question—I mean on the question of providing a carriage and horses."[1] The barouche was sent to the Hayes home in Fremont, Ohio, a month before President Garfield was shot by an assassin.[2]

Although it received many coats of paint, due to muddy roads in Ohio and extensive and steady use, the carriage was nevertheless well preserved. It has recently been restored by the Rutherford B. Hayes Library, Fremont, Ohio.

---

[1] Original Garfield Papers (letters received) Vol. 126, No. 78 (3 pp. fold) L. C.
[2] *Evening Star,* Washington, D.C., May 28, 1881.

Courtesy of the Lake County Historical Society

Carriage used by President James A. Garfield in Mentor, Ohio.

Chapter Twenty

Was carried to his final resting place
in a hearse that was one of
the finest vehicles of its kind
drawn by twelve black horses.

James A. Garfield

THE HORSES AND CARRIAGES of President Hayes were shipped back to him in June, 1881, when President Garfield's horses and carriage arrived at the White House. The new horses were bought by the President from Representative Updegraff and the carriage was built in New York.¹

President-elect Garfield had ridden to the Capitol to be inaugurated on March 4, 1881, in a four-horse barouche belonging to President Hayes. Bewhiskered President Hayes rode with him, as did members of the Senate Committee of Arrangements. The Columbia Commandery of Knight's Templar, of which Garfield was a member, formed a guard of honor. Vice-President-elect Arthur rode in a carriage behind Messrs. Garfield and Hayes.

The coachman was Albert Hawkins, a Negro who had served under several earlier Presidents. President Garfield kept the same horse and carriage which President Hayes had used and left behind. Writing to the President on February 7, 1881, General Garfield stated "I shall also be glad to accept your kind offer to use your horses and carriage a few weeks until I can find an outfit; if you still find it convenient to let me do so—But I beg you not to hesitate to tell me, if any other arrangement would suit you better."² On May 4, 1881, President Garfield wrote:

> When your son was here last he said it would not be inconvenient for you to leave your horses and carriage another month—and so I have not written you hitherto about shipping them.—It has been

a great favor to have them during March and April for it gave me time to make selection and purchase—I hope I have not detained them so long as to embarrass you. Please telegraph or write me when and how I shall ship them—I do not believe that any man in this office, has experienced so much helpful comradeship from his predecessor as I have.[3]

The carriage used by James A. Garfield in Mentor, Ohio before he went to the White House is still in existence and is now owned and exhibited by the Lake County Historical Society, at the James A. Garfield Home at Mentor. Another carriage claimed to have been used by Garfield is presently owned by Virgil L. Yarger, at Mansfield, Ohio.

Two months later, on July 2, 1881, the President was shot by an assassin, Charles J. Guiteau. Guiteau was immediately taken into custody and driven to prison in a five-glass landau built by Geissel and Bayha of Philadelphia.[4]

The President died on September 19, 1881. An elaborate funeral followed; fortunately a detailed description was published of the hearse which bore the remains from Cleveland to the last resting place:

The hearse or vehicle that was used in Cleveland for bearing our dead President to his last resting place attracted great attention, and was doubtless one of the finest vehicles of the kind ever improvised for a like service. It consisted of a platform, eight by sixteen feet, supported on four heavy truck wheels. From the edge of the platform to within an inch of the ground, heavy black drapery, bordered with silver fringe, was suspended. Immediately below and contiguous to the platform hung folds of heavy white silk, caught up with black silk cord. Two terrace steps lead up to the pall. Between the steps rools of immortelles run around the whole car. On each corner of the platform was a stand of flags draped in black. The arch canopy was supported by three columns on each side, covered with broadcloth and coiled garlands of immortelles, with capitals of Egyptian design. Immediately above the columns run a projecting cornice, with black and white roses. In the frieze, under which were hung festoons of heavy broadcloth and silver fringe, large wreaths of immortelles being displayed in the shape of lambrequins; on the four corners above the canopy, were black ostrich plumes—the whole crowned with a large urn wreathed with immortelles. This magnificent car was drawn by twelve black horses, four abreast, covered with heavy black blankets almost touching the ground, fringed with silver. On either side of each four horses was a colored groom—the same six did a like service at the funeral of the first martyr-President.[5]

[1] Feis, Ruth, *Mollie Garfield in the White House*, p. 76.
[2] Original Garfield papers, letters sent, Jan. 1—Sept. 5, 1881, p. 93, L.C.
[3] Original Garfield papers, letters sent, Jan. 1—Sept. 5, 1881, pp. 277-279.
[4] *The Hub*, Vol. 22, Dec. 1, 1881, p. 481.
[5] *The Carriage Monthly*, Vol. XVII, No. 7, Oct. 1881, p. 136.

Chapter Twenty-One

Rode in all the pomp and fashion of the day which his swanky carriage presented. His lap robe bore his initials.

Chester A. Arthur

PRESIDENT ARTHUR was displeased with the White House furnishings when he moved in, and most of them were promptly hauled away. The new look he effected extended also to his means of transportation. On December 7, 1881, after two and a half hectic months of refurnishing, the President, moved into the newly decorated mansion and was soon observed riding in the swankiest turnout in White House history. It was drawn by two perfectly matched mahogany bays with fine flowing manes and tails. These five-year-olds stood sixteen hands high. Their magnificent harness was mounted with plain silver. The dress blankets of heavy kersey and the coachman's lap robe of English box cloth were dark green and ornamented with the President's monogram. The President's lap-robe was of Labrador otter, lined with dark green silk which also bore the initials "C.A.A."[1]

The carriage, built by Brewster & Company of New York, was described as an elegant English-quarter pattern.[2] This dark green landau was trimmed with red, and the door panels were ornamented with the Arthur coat-of-arms.[3] The trimmings were of morocco and the cushions and doors were faced with heavy lace.

The whereabouts of this magnificent carriage in which President Arthur drove about the Nation's Capital is unknown today. One carriage in which both Presidents Arthur and Harrison rode is preserved at the Shelburne Museum in Vermont. This panel-boot victoria belonged to Governor Tilton of New Hampshire whom both presidents knew and visited.

[1] Furman, *White House Profile*, p. 235.
Hurd, *The White House*, p. 195.
Willets, *Inside History of the White House*, p. 430. *The Hub*, Vol. 23, p. 541—Vol. 24, p. 26.
[2] James B. Brewster & Co., were at 25th St., New York, and in 1882 moved to the corner of 5th Ave. & 42nd St. They had earlier supplied carriages for Presidents Garfield, Hayes, Grant, and Lincoln.
[3] *The Hub*, Vol. 23, p. 541.

Panel boot victoria used by Presidents Arthur and Harrison.

Courtesy of the Shelburne Museum, Inc.

Chapter Twenty-Two

One of his first duties after he assumed the office was to measure the hay in the White House stables and send a check to Ex-President Arthur for it.

Grover Cleveland

ON THE MORNING OF HIS INAUGURATION, Grover Cleveland was met at the White House by President Arthur. They rode to the Capitol in an open barouche lined with black and white robes and drawn by President Arthur's spanking bays. Coachman Albert Hawkins, who had driven for Presidents Grant, Hayes, Garfield, and Arthur, continued to drive during the Cleveland Administration.

One of President Cleveland's first acts after he assumed office was to measure the hay in the White House stables and send a check to ex-President Arthur for it.

Grover Cleveland was one of the very few Presidents who entered the White House as a bachelor. Shortly after becoming President, however, he proposed to Frances Folsom, and they were married in the White House on June 2, 1886. In the same year, the President purchased Red Top, a country house outside of Washington, D.C. On this property—sometimes referred to as Oak View—the President built a coach-house. In 1887 he purchased a light road wagon in which he commuted to Washington. He drove a pair of seal-brown horses which were left to be sold at Oak View after his first administration.[1]

The stables at the White House during Cleveland's terms of office contained five handsome vehicles: a custom-made black landau costing $2,000, received in 1885; a smart brougham, valued at $1,000; a victoria—Mrs. Cleveland's favorite carriage; a phaeton, made to order for $1,000 with a coachman's

101

rumble in the rear; and a surrey, sometimes called a buggy, which was a favorite vehicle of the President. [2]

The landau, or "Berlin landau," was built to order by a syndicate composed of A. S. Flandrau & Co., active Republican carriage builders from New York City, and B. Manville & Co., of New Haven, Connecticut. A contemporary description of this vehicle follows:

> The general design of this landau is standard and does not differ materially from others previously illustrated by us, but its proportions are well considered, and minute care has been bestowed upon the execution of the details, and the selection of thoroughly first-class materials, which combine to give it a degree of elegance that no mere novelty of design can effect. It is quite plain throughout. All the moldings, so generally placed, are painted black, with the single exception of the one around the valance on the seat-frame of the driver's-seat. The door handles are of a peculiar finish. The center of the handle is slightly boxed out on the surface to within 3/16 in. from the outside edge, and the space is filled in with black enameled rubber, the silver-plated portion forming a bead. This combination of black and silver produces a quiet and elegant appearance. The lamps, which are large but of plain pattern, show excellent workmanship. The inside plating especially is done exceedingly well.
>
> Straight-grained French leather is used for the top and covering of the neck panel. The material used for the interior trimming consists of French morocco, and Wulfing's best cloth. The broad-lace is of the latest pattern, and hand-made by the well-known house of F. J. Schmid, of this city.
>
> The body is of the regular English-quarter pattern. The quarters are of good size, giving comfortable seat-room. The corner-pillars are made of bent wood as usual. The standing-pillars are secured to the rockers by screws. The screws are inserted from the inside. A half-round bead is worked on the outside of the standing-pillars below the panels, near the front, and on the rear face. The moldings on the body are of the size now generally applied to such vehicles, and finish with a square bead on the inside edge. The size of the bead is about 3/16 x 1/8 in. The beds of the front gear are swept forward 3-1/2 in. The rear axle is cranked 2 in., to obtain the proper opening of the springs.
>
> Finish.—Painting of the body, quarters, doors and back panels, Dutch-pink green; and moldings, boot-panels and other parts of the body black. The moldings are striped on the inside edge with a fine line of apple-green. The gearing is painted with the same color as that used on the body panels, striped with a broad stripe and two fine lines of black.
>
> The trimming material is dark green French morocco for the backs and cushion tops, and dark green cloth for the upper and lower quarters, backs, doors, head-lining, and driver's-seat. The upholstering on the backs is laid out in large diamonds, which figure is also applied to the cushion tops and lower quarters. The tufts used are dark green, and of good size. The arm-pieces are covered

with morocco, edged by a welt of the same material. The cushion fronts are covered with broad-lace of the latest pattern, known as "cut lace." No falls are used. The heel boards are covered with cloth, lightly padded, and edged with broad-lace. Five tufts are inserted for a finish, namely: one in the center, and the others at equal distances from the broad-lace, or about 2 in. Creases run from the center tuft to those in the corners, and materially enhance the appearance of the door trimming. A card-case is attached to the off-side door, covered with dark green morocco and edged with a very light silver-plated bead. On the near-side door another case is attached, containing a looking-glass. The finish of this case resembles that on the other door. The driver's-seat is trimmed plain, as is customary. The fall has a raiser of considerable width, inclosed by two lines of stitching. The width of the raiser and stitching is about 2 in. Carpet, French moquette, in dark green color, with cut figures.

Mountings, silver. The axle-caps are black enameled on the front, and the firm name of the builders is engraved on the same in raised letters, silver-mounted. [3]

Of eight horses domiciled in the White House stables five belonged to the President. Four were brown bays, three of which were perfectly matched. Two of these were for Mrs. Cleveland and two for the President, although all four were used together on special public occasions. The three other horses—furnished by the Government—were used on official business by the President's secretaries. Coachman Hawkins and Beverly Lemos rode on the box. [4]

President Cleveland frequently enjoyed a drive in his landau with Mrs. Cleveland or with his secretary, Daniel Lamont.

In 1889 Cleveland accompanied President-elect Harrison to the Capitol in his landau drawn by the four bays, Harrison on the left side of the outgoing President.

Upon his return to the White House for his second term, in 1893, President Cleveland was greeted cordially by the outgoing President. They drove together to the inauguration in an open barouche again drawn by four horses.

One month before the inauguration, Mrs. Cleveland had ordered from W. M. Healey & Co., Broadway and Fifty-first Street, New York, a new phaeton for her own use and a new landau for the President. The phaeton was delivered shortly after the inauguration and the landau in May. A contemporary description of the landau follows:

It is a big round-bodied landau of the type in use about twenty-five years ago. The lines of construction taper from the center of the body to the footboard and to the scroll springs in the rear. The body, built of ash, poplar and cherry, is painted a dark olive green, with black mouldings picked out with fine apple-green lines. The running gear is black, decorated with a half-inch line of apple-green on the hub, felloe and spokes. The door panels and back panels have "G.

C." in monogram, also on apple-green. The top of the landau is of heavily enameled tanned leather, divided crosswise in the middle so that it may fold down tight to the body and make an open carriage for Summer use. The few bits of ornamentation are of silver, the door handles being chased. There are silver guards to the footman's steps and four narrow silver bands about the stems and tops of the lamps. The lamps are of "cylinder pattern," and have each four panes of three-eighth-inch beveled plate glass, held in by silver mountings. The front springs are of the elliptic order, and the rear springs what is termed scroll style. There is a double fifth wheel to give increased strength. The coachman's seat has a double rail and skirts and is trimmed with dark green boxcloth. Beneath this seat is a cupboard for the rubber aprons and seat covers. The pole is of Vermont ash and is padded to protect the horses' sides. All the spring heads are rubber packed to give more freedom to the spring and reduce the amount of jarring.

The inside width of the carriage from door to door is forty-five inches, and the outside length six feet. The doorway is made extra wide, and the door, by means of a compass hinge, opens out further than the door of an ordinary landau. The cane bottom seats are fitted with extra thick cushions of dark green morocco leather, and on the sides of the seats are projecting ledges like the arms of a chair. The glass of the front and sides is crystal plate and is one-fourth of an inch thick. The carriage weighs 1,590 pounds and cost $1,800. [5]

In his final official appearance, in 1897, Cleveland rode to the Capitol in an open carriage drawn by four bay horses. He subsequently returned to private life at Princeton, where he enjoyed daily rides with his wife in his carriage. His stables at Princeton contained a handsome pair of horses and he employed a coachman. [6]

Of all the carriages used by President Cleveland, only one is known to have survived. This is a brougham used after his retirement at the dedication of the J. Sterling Morton Monument in 1905. It is presently located at Arbor Lodge State Historical Park, Nebraska City, Nebraska.

---

[1] Nevans, *Grover Cleveland—A Study in Courage,* p. 213.
[2] Colman, *White House Gossip,* p. 228.
Willets, *Inside History of the White House,* p. 430.
Singleton, *The Story of the White House,* Vol. 2, p. 209.
[3] *The Hub,* Vol. 27, June 1, 1885, p. 147—"The dimensions of the carriage were: Width of body at the hinge-pillar, 54 in.; ditto lock-pillar, 54 in.; ditto front, 45 in.; ditto rear, 45-1/4 in.; and ditto toeboard, 35-1/2 in. Turn-under, 3 in. Rocker-plates, 4 x 1/2 in.; fastened with 2 in. No. 20 screws. Height of wheels: front, 2 ft. 11 in., and rear, 3 ft. 10 in., without the tire. Depth of rims, 1-5/8 in. Number of spokes, 10 and 12. The spokes have no stagger. Hubs: front, 6-1/4 in., and rear 6-1/2 in. diameter. Size of front bands for the front hubs, 4-1/4 in., and back 5 in., inside diameter. Front bands for the rear hubs, 4-3/8 in. Back bands, 5-1/8 in., inside diameter. Length of front bands, 2-1/8 in. Length of hubs, 8-1/4 in. Tire, 1-3/8 x 3/8 in.; roundedge steel.

"The front springs are elliptic, 41 in. long, from out to out, with 10 in. opening over all. Width of steel, 1-3/4 in. Number of plates, five, namely: the first three No. 2, and the last two No. 3 steel Holes apart on the top half, 3-3/4 in. Size of holes, 5/16 in. The rear springs are platform. The side-springs are 43 in. long, from out to out, with 9 in. opening over all. Width of steel, 1-3/4 in. Number of plates, four, namely: the first No. 1, the second No. 2, the third No. 3, and the last No. 4 steel. Holes apart on the top half, 3-1/2 in. size of holes, 5/16 in. The cross-spring is 46-1/4 in., from center to center, with 4-1/2 in. set over all. Width of steel, 1-3/4 in. Number of plates, four, namely: the first No. 1, the next No. 2, and the last two No. 3 steel. Axles, 1-7/16 in., Collinge patent. Track: front, 4 ft. 5-1/2 in., and rear, 5 ft. 2 in., from out to out."

[4] Colman, *White House Gossip,* p. 228.
[5] *The Blacksmith and Wheelwright,* Vol. 27-28, May 1893, p. 262.
[6] Nevans, *Grover Cleveland,* p. 731. Martin, *After the White House,* p. 330.

Landau built by W. M. Healy & Co., New York in 1893.

From the Blacksmith and Wheelwright, N.Y.

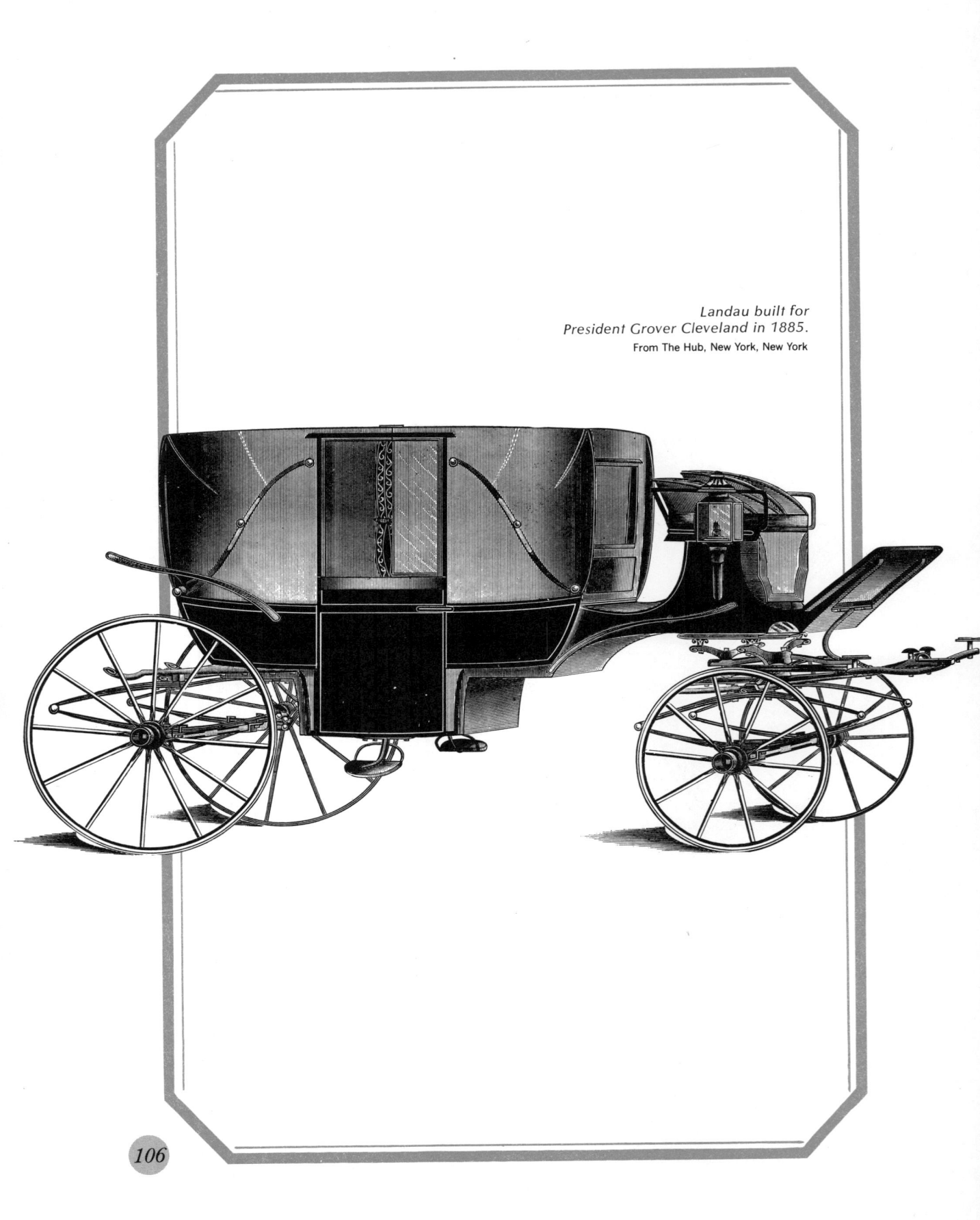

*Landau built for
President Grover Cleveland in 1885.*
From The Hub, New York, New York

Chapter Twenty-Three

**Usually went riding
from 4 to 6 o'clock each afternoon,
afterwhich he returned for dinner.**

Benjamin Harrison

PRESIDENT HARRISON BROUGHT WITH HIM for use in his inauguration an elegant landau which he had purchased from Studebaker Brothers for $2,000. This carriage became the official "state coach" of the administration. Dark green like Cleveland's carriage, this landau was, however, without initials, monograms, or crest. The harness was ornamented with plain silver mountings. A contemporary account described it as:

> ... a full leather landau. The top is thrown back by springs hidden from view but controlled by the driver. The body panels are painted a dark green, the moldings and boot are painted black, and the wheels and other gearing a dark green, striped with three lines of black. The outside trimmings are large square lamps with silver frames and beveled crystal plates, silver door handles and axle caps, and silver top and seat moldings. The driver's seat is upholstered in green cloth with rubber board and apron. The top has a crown cover, and the pole straps silver loops. The inside trimmings are of the most expensive green cloth and lace, but by desire of the President are exceedingly plain. The inside mountings are of ebony, silver, and morocco leather. The first thing that strikes the observer is the exceeding neatness of finish. It is difficult to understand how it could be made so and at the same time observe the President's wish for simplicity and plainness. [1]

The other vehicles also made by Studebaker Brothers and brought to the White House by President Harrison were simple, strong, and elegant. His favorite was a high, heavy buggy made to his order. It contained a broad box; its top covered only the front seat and was generally thrown back. The makers termed

Buggy used by President Benjamin Harrison both in Washington and in Indianapolis.
Courtesy of the Studebaker Museum

Brougham built by Studebaker Brothers for President Benjamin Harrison and used by the family until 1911.
Courtesy of the Benjamin Harrison Home

this buggy a "mail phaeton." The President preferred to ride in this vehicle without a coachman or footman, holding the reins himself with great confidence. He usually rode each afternoon, just before dinner, accompanied either by Mrs. Harrison, Secretary Halford, Mrs. Dimmick, his wife's niece, or his daughter, Mrs. McKee. Occasionally a Cabinet member accompanied him for a confidential talk.

Mrs. Harrison used a brougham the President bought from the Studebaker Brothers for $2,000. It was designed by Joseph Kopcsay, in the same color and finish as the President's landau. A drop seat was specially designed to accommodate the President's three little grandchildren. At the President's death the brougham became the property of his sister, who left it to her daughter, Mrs. Lillie Eaton, a resident of the old Harrison homestead near North Bend, Ohio. Mrs. Eaton presented the brougham to her husband's friend, C. L. Hayes after 1900.[2] It is today in the Studebaker Brothers Museum.

The buggy or run-about used by President Harrison while driving to and from his Indianapolis law office is in the President's home in Indianapolis. It was stored in the old barn after Harrison's death. When the dilapidated barn was torn down and the home restored, the buggy was repainted and stored on the third floor where it now remains. According to tradition this buggy was shipped to Washington, D.C., and used occasionally, but it was never as popular with the President as his "mail phaeton."

Albert Hawkins, Negro coachman for the Harrisons, had been in charge of the White House stables for a quarter of a century. During the Harrison Administration, the stables were occupied by six matched cherry bay horses, which stood sixteen and a half hands. Four of the animals were family horses, all Kentucky thoroughbreds, named Abdullah, Billy, Lexington, and John. In addition to the Harrison team, there were three office horses used for delivering messages and packages to various government departments.

The President sometimes drove with two bays, which on occasion were noted to be shaggy and ungroomed. In general, however, the White House horses were well cared for, and the family was often complimented on its fine horses and handsome carriages.[3]

---

[1] *The Blacksmith and Wheelwright,* Vol. 19, No. 4, Apr. 1889, p. 246.
[2] *The Vehicle Dealer,* Vol. 9, July, 1906, p. 248.
[3] Information concerning the Harrison equipage is to be found in *The Hub News,* Vol. 1, No. 42, Feb. 24, 1892, p. 5. *The Hub,* Vol. 33, June, 1891, p. 182; also Vol. 35, Apr. 1893, p. 52. Carpenter, *Carp's Washington,* p. 304. Colman, *White House Gossip,* p. 210.

From The Hub, New York, New York

Carriage built by Studebaker Brothers and used by President William McKinley in Canton, Ohio when he returned there for visits from the White House.

Chapter Twenty-Four

"President McKinley has tasted the joys
of a ride in an automobile.
He was seen early this week in a steam carriage
of F. O. Stanley, the inventor of the Locomobile."

William McKinley

ON MARCH 4, 1897, President-elect William McKinley and President Cleveland rode to the Capitol in an open carriage drawn by four bays. After the ceremony they rode back to the White House together.

In January 1897, President McKinley had ordered three vehicles—a brougham, a landau, and a cabriolet, also termed a victoria—for his White House stables. The vehicles were built by C. P. Kimball & Co. of Chicago, Illinois. A contemporary account described the order as follows:

> President McKinley will ride around Washington in carriages built in Chicago.... He has sent $5,000 to C. P. Kimball & Co. to pay for this part of the equipment of the White House stables....
>
> It was decided by the McKinley household that three vehicles would be necessary. A cabriolet will be needed for dry days and turns along the avenue, a landau for rain and society trips, and a brougham would carry all the members of the family. All are to be made for two horses, and the instructions to the builders were to spare nothing to make them rich—not showy. They are to outshine the old one-horse chaise, with its two seats, which has carried many an aspirant from the station in Canton to the Mecca since election.
>
> The brougham will be done in green morocco and satin.
>
> The cabriolet will be furnished in green morocco and cloth.
>
> The landau will be same as the cabriolet, with a little difference in the quality of material.
>
> All the trimmings are to be silver—the first open declaration for silver on the part of the Major, and that is not for coinage.
>
> The vehicles are to be fitted with rubber tires, all the springs being especially constructed to make the riding without the suggestion of a jolt.

> *The harnesses are to bear silver ornaments; the bits and buckles to be of the same metal.*
>
> *The windows will have pneumatic rims to make them air-tight and still easy to move.*
>
> *The pole sockets are to be done in silver, padded and trimmed with rims like the windows.*
>
> *This completes the items in the contract. It was mentioned in the order that great care should be taken with all the details, and C. P. Kimball & Co. promised to make the rigs as right as a dress suit is right. They are to be sent to the capital as soon as completed. "A carriage must be just right, or it is all wrong," he said last night. "It must follow rules as rigidly as an evening suit." The President-elect placed his order in Chicago because he ... has probably learned that the center of the carriage trade is here...* [1]

The landau harness for the team was also furnished by C. P. Kimball & Co. and is described as "a full 1 3/8 in. trace, bradoon swivel check, Buxton bit, hames, all large buckles, terrets, etc., full silver; small buckles leather covered. It is made of the best American harness leather, and with the neatness and high finish which is characteristic of an American gentleman's coach harness." [2] The brougham harness was light 1 3/8-inch trace also, but plainly finished.

When Mr. McKinley assumed the Presidency he left in Canton, Ohio only one old white horse and an old chaise with a dusty top. Accordingly, he ordered Studebaker to build a new carriage which he could use on visits to his home town. In this new Studebaker carriage the President rode to the railway station enroute for Buffalo, New York, where he was later assassinated. The carriage is now in the Studebaker Museum.

Many stories develop about vehicles ordered for Presidential use. Although President McKinley walked more than he drove, stories about his carriages were widespread. A contemporary writer described one of the Chicago-built McKinley carriages in this manner:

> *The President has bought a new trap, which he initiated to-day. It is constructed on the most fashionable lines, is strictly up to date, embodies all that is modern, including rubber tires, meets all the requirements of society fold and, altogether, is the smartest turnout ever owned by a Chief Magistrate of the United States. It is for the exclusive use of Mr. and Mrs. McKinley. There is one seat in front and a single seat behind for the footman.*
>
> *The trap was not purchased for the purpose of ostentation, nor because it is stylish, but because it will afford the President more opportunity for outdoor exercise. With this rig he handles the reins himself and thus gets the full benefit of his drives. Mr. McKinley enjoys driving when he guides the horses himself. He is a horseman of no mean ability, as he proved last winter when he drove a spirited span hitched to a cutter.*

> With Mrs. McKinley at his side, he thoroughly enjoyed the innovation, and so did she. They took a spin along Connecticut Avenue, the most fashionable thoroughfare in Washington. Coming and going, were traps, carriages and rigs of every description, but none pleased the fastidious eye more than the Presidential turnout.
>
> The President enjoys his trap the more because Mrs. McKinley can share the pleasure with him. Some months ago he frequently took horseback rides, but he could not have the company of his wife, whose comfort is always his first thought.[3]

She was suffering from epilepsy during her entire White House life, and the President kept close by Mrs. McKinley's side because of her condition. She was his first thought, and when he was shot in Buffalo, one of his first utterances was "be careful how you break the news to Ida."

When the landau and brougham were delivered in March 1897, the following description appeared in a carriage journal:

> An examination of these carriages shows them to be up to the latest and most acceptable patterns, and confirms the position taken by The Hub regarding the ultra-fashionable vehicles of this class. They are the embodiment of plainness, harmonious in outlines, and artistic in every detail that tends to make a perfect vehicle. When the order was placed Mr. McKinley specially requested that the colors used should be quiet in tone, and as far as possible they would be constructed of American materials. In accordance with this request the builders constructed the bodies on the lines of their regular work. The axles were made by the Dalzell Axle Co., South Engremout, Mass., and have solid flanges and wrought boxes. The springs were fitted with rubber heads; the leather by Halsey & Smith, of Newark, N.J., from imported French hides, having a surface finish superior to any foreign finished leather. The cloth, which is dark green in shade, was made by the Waterloo Woolen Manufacturing Co., New York; the colors and varnished by Valentine & Company, New York.
>
> Both carriages are upholstered in dark green morocco and cloth. Handles, plain bar pattern, silver mounted. Square lamp with clamp socket. Silver bead around the glass, all the rest black.
>
> The body panels are painted rifle green, with black moldings. Running gears, rifle green, striped single broad line of black. Monogram on crest panel, McK., in green.
>
> Splinter bar fitted with Wheat's patent trace posts. Wheels with rubber tires.
>
> The inside of the carriage is fitted with bell for calling the coachman, hand mirror, card case, foot cushions and other usual fittings, the brougham having, in addition, shopping pockets and toilet case.
>
> The poles are fitted with polished steel crabs, that of the brougham being fitted with the builder's patent rubber lined pole sockets to prevent rattle, and their design of ventilator for the inside, so arranged that the windows may be kept closed and yet have perfect circulation of air in the carriage.[4]

From The Hub, New York, New York

President William McKinley's brougham, 1897.

*President
William McKinley's
cabriolet, 1897.*
From The Hub, New York, New York

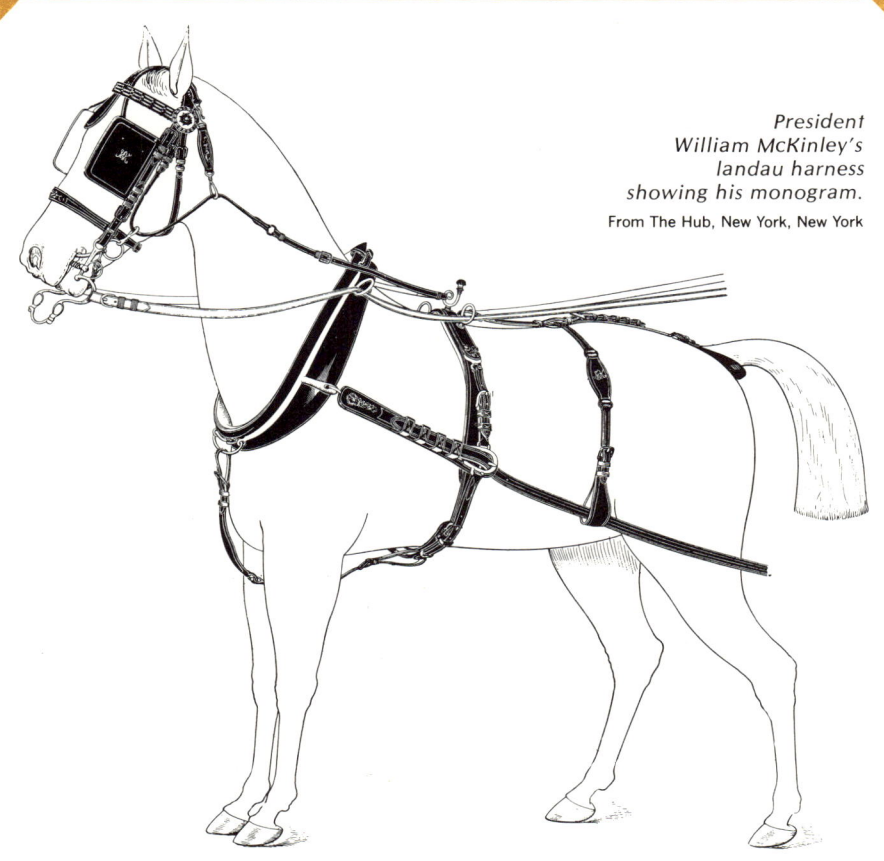

President William McKinley's landau harness showing his monogram.
From The Hub, New York, New York

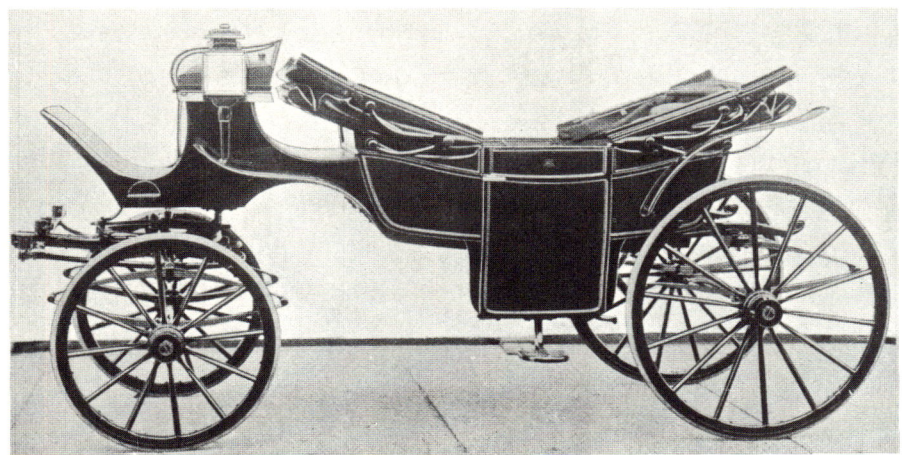

Landau built for President William McKinley in 1897.   From The Hub, New York, New York

When the cabriolet was delivered in April, 1897, it was of the same color as the other two carriages and was made of American materials. The back seat was trimmed with dark green goatskin, while the driver's seat and top lining was of waterloo cloth. [5]

Each Sunday at ten minutes before eleven the President drove to church in his carriage drawn by black horses. An evening drive with his wife was his usual relaxation.

In 1899, President McKinley experienced his first ride in an automobile. A contemporary account recorded it in this fashion:

> *[President McKinley]* was seen early this week in the steam carriage of F. O. Stanley, the inventor of the Locomobile. Now that the horseless carriage has won the approval of the Chief Magistrate, its popularity will gain a decided impetus.
>
> The Locomobile Co. seem to be the only ones who appreciate what a splendid market Washington is for motor vehicles. Washington teems with wealthy people who are seeking some healthful diversion or amusement, and who would willingly invest in automobiles if they could see them; but the idea of ordering machines by mail without being able to see for themselves what they will do and what they look like does not appeal to them. [6]

During the summer of 1901, the President and Mrs. McKinley took a three-month vacation from Washington and returned for a rest to their beloved Canton. Myron T. Herricks' "horseless buggy" and driver were put at their disposal. [7] During their stay in Canton, the President decided to take his first open-road drive in an automobile. The driver, Zib Davis, an old Cantonian employed making cars in Cleveland, afforded the President much joy in this adventure as long as he was heading down straight roads. At corners, however, the President would stiffen up and tightly hold the seat and arm. [8]

Mr. McKinley's 1899 automobile ride may distinguish him as the first presidential automobile passenger. Although Grover Cleveland was President in 1893 when Frank Duryea built the first American-made, gasoline-powered motor vehicle, Mr. Cleveland never rode in an automobile while he occupied the White House. Until President Harding's inauguration no President rode in an automobile to important and dignified ceremonies.

On September 6, 1901, President McKinley left the Milburn home in Buffalo for the Pan-American Exposition in the Milburn's carriage, while Mrs. McKinley remained at the Milburn home. She never returned to the White House after the President's death. The Milburn carriage was in Canada until 1960, but it has since fallen apart from neglect. In 1938 the carriage oil lamps were removed; until recently they were in the possession of Cecil E. Lasby, Turkey Point,

Ontario, Canada. The carriage was a landau of a deep wine color with a black leather top. The upholstery was of a wine broadcloth to match the exterior. The Buffalo and Erie County Historical Society and the Automobile Manufacturers Association, Inc. have photographs of the automobile ambulance which conveyed the President from the Temple of Music to the hospital. Also in the Historical Society is a photograph of the hearse which conveyed his body to the train.

[1] *The Hub,* Vol. 6, p. 921, Jan. 27, 1897.
[2] *The Hub,* Vol. 39, May, 1897, p. 103.
[3] Willets, *Inside History of the White House,* pp. 430, 431.
[4] *The Hub,* Vol. 38, Mar., 1897, p. 791.
[5] *The Hub,* Vol. 39, Apr., 1897, p. 24.
[6] *The Horseless Age,* New York, Nov. 22, 1899.
[7] Jones, *Homes of the American Presidents,* p. 158.
[8] *Motor Review,* July 18, 1901.

Courtesy of the Buffalo and Erie County Historical Society
McKinley funeral leaving Milburn House, Delaware Avenue.

*Brougham used by
President Theodore Roosevelt
while occupying
the White House.*
Courtesy of The Henry Ford Museum, Dearborn, Michigan

Chapter Twenty-Five

"I came to the inauguration
in this horse-drawn vehicle and
I will leave in it."

Theodore Roosevelt

THEODORE ROOSEVELT HAD extensive stables at Sagamore Hill before he became President. As early as 1887, he had two riding horses. One named "Sagamore" was a magnificent hunter, and "Caution" doubled as a buggy-horse. Two "wooly horses" were used for farm work. "Diamond" and "Pickle," the children's riding horses, were often hitched to a pony-cart which Alice Roosevelt's Grandfather Lee gave Mrs. Edith Roosevelt for the Roosevelt children. A pony presented to Alice by her Grandfather Lee was named "General Grant" after the pony Roosevelt had had as a boy. Frank Hall was in charge of the Sagamore Hill stables, and a man named Seaman was the coachman. During the Spanish-American War, Edith bought a new horse which she named "Cuba." When Theodore Roosevelt rode in the Battle of San Juan he used a pony named "Texas," which he brought to Sagamore Hill after the war. In addition to horses and ponies, the stables contained a two-seated tasseled surrey, known in the family as the "express wagon"; a two-seated buckboard, in which they went to church; an uncovered carriage; and a three-seated wagon. [1]

When President McKinley was assassinated Theodore Roosevelt was at a mountain camp in the Adirondacks of New York. As soon as the news reached him, the Vice President set out for Buffalo. Theodore Roosevelt was unofficially President while he was riding toward the railroad station in a surrey, for McKinley was already dead. This surrey is still in existence; and is now in the Adirondacks Museum.

During President Roosevelt's Administration the equipage at the White House consisted of a landau, a brougham, a basket surrey, a buggy, and a phaeton (the so-called uncovered carriage) which had been in the Roosevelt family for many years. In addition the Quartermaster Corps purchased a victoria, which completed the stable ensemble.[2] Two carriage teams, six riding horses for the family, four horses for Secretary Loeb, and three office horses filled the stables to capacity.[3] The President usually drove only two horses with a Negro coachman and footman attending. Through the Roosevelt Administration, White House livery consisted of a blue coat, white doeskin trousers, high boots, and top hat with a red, white, and blue cockade.

An illustration of one carriage team purchased in 1905 and the following account appeared in a contemporary publication:

> *The Spokesman is enabled to present a portrait of the peerless match pair of horses, which was recently purchased through the dealers mentioned. They were bought in Goshen, Ind., by M. H. Tichenor & Co. of Chicago, who had been commissioned by the President to secure the Team.*
>
> *Riley T. and Billy H. are 16 hands high, blood bays, weigh in the same notch at 2,500 pounds, and are matched in carriage, manners, style, action and speed. Each has a white hind foot and a small star in the forehead. Judges of horse flesh pronounce them the best team they ever saw. They are five years old this spring.*
>
> *Billy H. was sired by Prince Exem (2:16¼), he by Tom Exem, he by Oward. The dam of Billy H. was by a son of Magna Carta. Riley T. is by Billy T., he by Bassett M., whose dam was by Hawptach. The dam of Riley T. was by Greenbrier (2:22).*[4]

A 1902 brougham drawn by two horses was purchased during his administration and used by President Roosevelt on many official occasions at the White House. The brougham was kept until 1928; it was then sold by the government to The Henry Ford Museum and Greenfield Village at Dearborn, Michigan, where it is now located.

Roosevelt's victoria, a type of vehicle named after England's Queen and considered the social vehicle of Europe and America during the late 19th and early 20th centuries, was manufactured by John C. Harvey Company, Buffalo, N.Y.[5] This vehicle was taken from storage and used by President Wilson during World War I when gasoline was scarce. Mrs. Coolidge used it on two occasions for drives through the city and parks. Both the brougham and victoria were used for their marketing by the White House housekeepers, Mrs. Jaffray during the Wilson Administration, and later Miss Riley. The victoria was disposed of by the United States Government at the same time as the brougham.[6] At that time, Tom, the old Negro coachman, sought other employment and the housekeepers

President Theodore Roosevelt's favorite riding horse. From The Vehicle Dealer.

Courtesy of Smithsonian Institution

White House victoria used by President Theodore Roosevelt and later by President Woodrow Wilson.

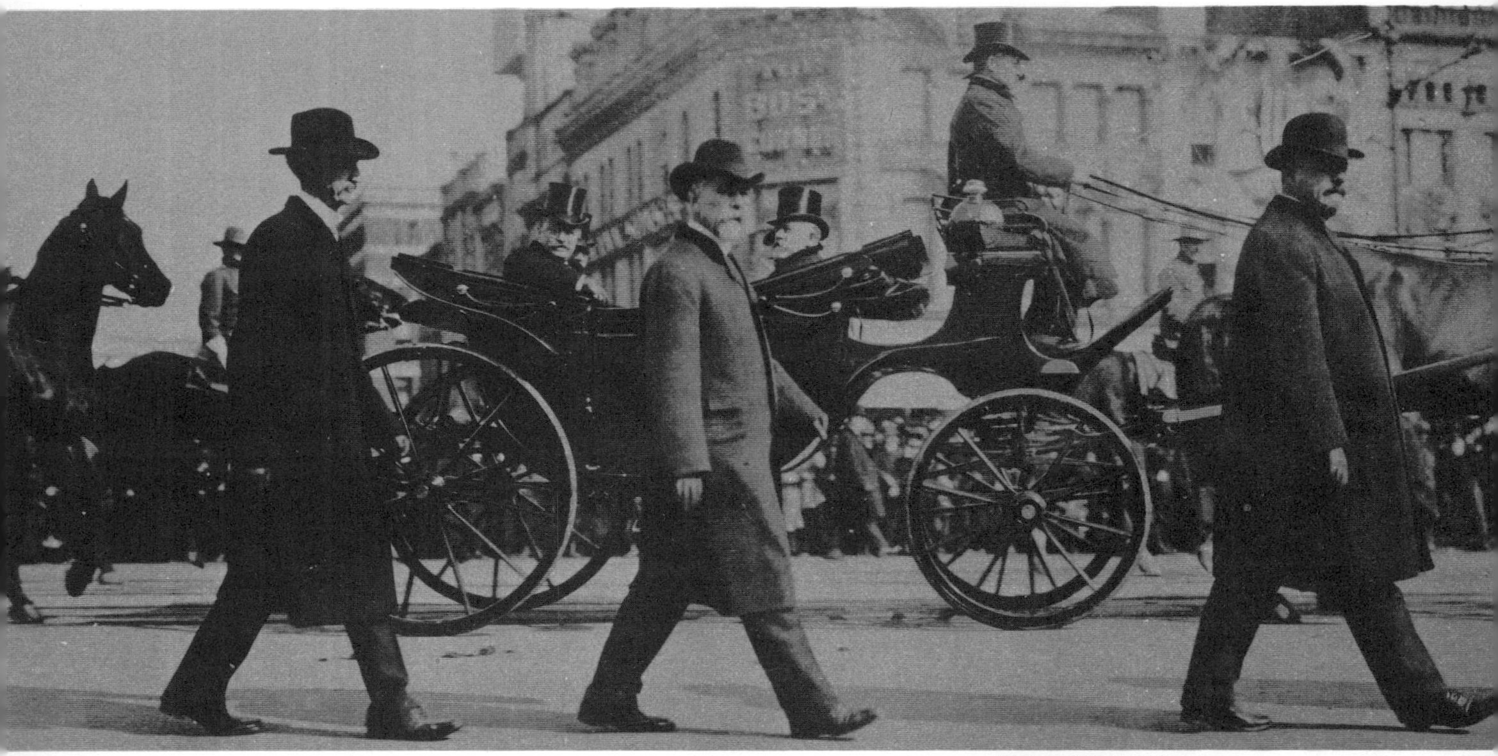

Courtesy of Library of Congress

President Theodore Roosevelt on his way to the Capitol for his inauguration in 1905.

From The Vehicle Dealer

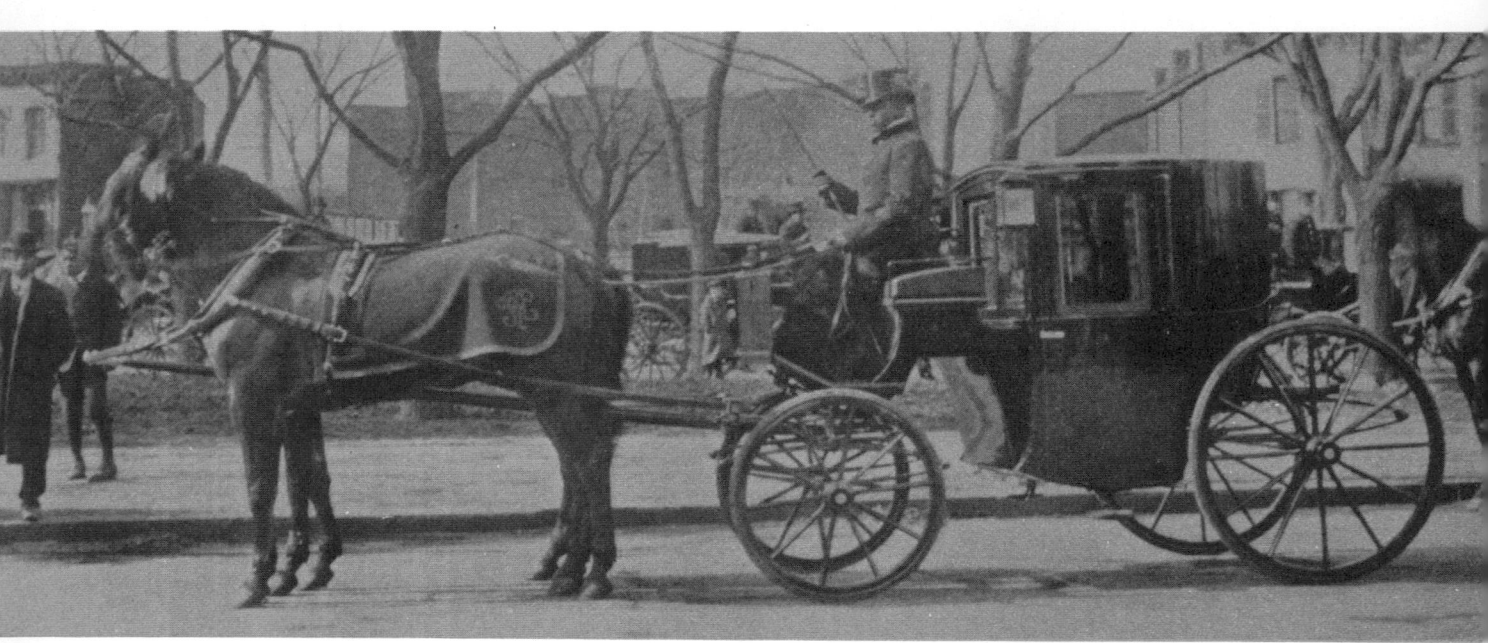

President Roosevelt's brougham and horses bearing the monogrammed harness, used by the President for riding in and about Washington.

changed to automotive transportation. The victoria and a double set of harness were transferred in 1928 from the War Department to the Smithsonian Institution. The disposal of these two carriages ended the era of horse-drawn vehicles at the White House.

Mrs. Roosevelt's favorite vehicle was the surrey. Its pattern was severely plain with angles rather than curves predominating.[7] Its present whereabouts is unknown.

A buggy, which was also referred to as "a small open trap," was used by Ethel, Roosevelt's daughter.

In August, 1906, President Roosevelt purchased for use at Oyster Bay a three-seated platform spring-wagon. Edward A. Hofheins, representative of the Keystone Wagon Works, Reading, Pennsylvania, received the order through McReynolds Sons of Washington, D.C. Known as No. 71 of the Keystone line, the wagon had removable seats for six passengers, was trimmed in tan corduroy, and had blue gearing without striping.[8]

Although the President did not use automobiles frequently, probably because of his great love of horses, he did on several occasions ride in them during his term of office. In one instance he participated in a free advertising scheme planned by A. P. Warner, developer of the speedometer. Mr. Warner sent a demonstration car to several cities, including Washington. It was driven slowly past the White House; when the President spotted it, he rushed out to inspect the giant speedometer. He was so intrigued that he got into the car and rode around the block.[9]

The Roosevelt family often enjoyed rides together. A reporter gave the following account of their 1903 Christmas evening:

> The Roosevelt children on Christmas afternoon paid a visit to the home of Captain Cowles, whose wife is a sister of the President, and there they had some part in the Christmas tree prepared particularly for their seven-year-old cousin. This tree, too, was a simple affair, and the occasion proved essentially homelike.
>
> After a few hours at the Cowles residence the basket surrey and another carriage from the White House stables appeared before the door to take the President's family for a drive into the country. Everybody went. Both vehicles were filled. There was even some rivalry among the children for seats. This outing afforded the quiet and refreshment, after a day crowded with pleasures and interests, which the entire household seemed to need. The President's driver did not need to be told in which direction to turn the horses' heads. The deepest woods which can be reached in a few miles are usually sought for, and especially was this true on Christmas afternoon. Washington is fortunate among American cities in having with a half-hour's drive forests so dense, penetrated only by such narrow coun-

try roads as to disguise every suggestion that a great city is almost lurking from behind the next bend in the highway.

The carriages rolled back in early twilight. The children, after their usual light supper, were ready to enjoy sound slumber, while their parents dressed for dinner. Their guests were the family friends rather than members of the official circles who, on formal occasions, are invited to the White House. The President's desire was to make Christmas throughout a day of the home and of home friends.[10]

Predictably, outdoorsman Roosevelt was involved in both carriage and horse accidents. One such accident occurred on September 3, 1902. During the late summer of 1902, the President decided to tour New England for about ten days. Secretary Cortelyou and the White House Secret Service men accompanied him. On the last day of the tour when he and Massachusetts Governor Murray Crane were driving to a meeting near Pittsfield, his carriage had a collision with a trolley car. The President suffered only a swollen lip, injured hand and leg, and various severe and painful bruises, but one of the Secret Service men, "Big Bill" Craig, was killed instantly. Immediately the press pounced upon the incident for a big story. The Associated Press rushed its Washington representative to Oyster Bay in time for the President's arrival. Despite his injuries he continued his tour, making his final speech that evening at Bridgeport. The President was so annoyed and embarrassed about the incident that he refused to let the story use his name.[11]

Archibald Butt, Aide-de-camp for both Roosevelt and Taft, reported that by this time the White House stables were equipped with telephones. In 1908 Butt described the Roosevelt horses: "Larry" was Butt's personal horse. "Rosewell" was the President's favorite jumper until an injury to the horse forced him to get a replacement. He named the new horse "Georgia," because the day he tried her out was like a hot Georgia day. Writing to Archie Butt, the President said, "I cannot tell you how much I like Georgia. I never had such a feeling of perfect safety on an animal before."[12] "Rosewell" recovered and was sold at auction for $500 to a Harvard colleague of the President, Mr. De Naige. Two hours after the sale Senator Frank Kellogg, then Ambassador to England, offered $100 more.[13] For $600 the President's mare, "Audrey," was sold to Secretary Straus to be used by Mrs. Straus. Other horses in the stable were named "Yagenka," "Jacko Root," "Renown," "Bleistein," "Wyoming," "Rusty," "Grey Dawn," and the tiny Icelandic pony, "Algonquin."

An accident involving the President in June 1908, was reported in a letter from Archie Butt as follows:

You are right in your surmise that the horse that dumped the President was the one I had written you about.

From The Hub, New York, N.Y.

Basket-type surrey, Mrs. Theodore Roosevelt's favorite vehicle.

From The Hub, New York, N.Y.

Old style phaeton used for many years by the Theodore Roosevelt family.

I had purchased the horse in Philadelphia and the animal seemed perfectly kind and gentle. I rode him through the park, up and down the embankments, into the water and through the fords, and he did nothing to excite my suspicions. So I reported to the President that he was safe, and that afternoon he ordered him saddled for himself. It seems that the horse balked when the President tried to take him through the creek and wheeled about to come up the bank.

That the President likes to have his own way with horses as well as men is accepted now as a fact, so he tried to wheel the horse about again, which he succeeded in doing, but the horse wheeled again, and in doing so went over backward and both fell into the creek. Fortunately, the water was deep at that point and no great harm was done, but it would have been serious had the water been more shallow. Unfortunately, some people were near and reported the matter to the newspapers, so greatly exaggerated accounts of the accident were published.

thought the President would be chagrined, as he is rather proud of his horsemanship, and he has a right to be, for he now rides a different horse every day, and horses, moreover, that he knows nothing about, and has to rely on me or someone else for the fact that it is safe. Our Government is most parsimonious as to the allowances for the White House. As long as men were Presidents who only wanted horses to drive from one place to another, and cared nothing for horseflesh itself, the allowances for the stables were ample, but the President has to furnish his own mounts, and when they are sick, as they frequently are, he has to beg, borrow, or as he says, steal from the Quartermaster's Department for a mount.[14]

In 1911 a group from Galveston, Texas, who had served under "the Rough Rider," presented the Colonel with a saddle valued at $500. This hand-made saddle was of Texas leather, Oklahoma lumber, and was ornamented with New Mexico gold. Originally the men had planned to present the saddle to Colonel Roosevelt upon his return from Africa, but it was not completed in time. They also spoke of presenting him with a cow pony from the Doherty Ranch if he would visit Texas for a hunt.[15] Although no confirmation of this is in the records, President Roosevelt may well have accepted the offer because he so loved to hunt.

The saddlemaker is not known, but a periodical in 1933 carried a photograph of Jose Quidada of San Jose, California, who had earlier made a saddle for Theodore Roosevelt.[16]

There are two buggies of the period at Theodore Roosevelt's Sagamore Hill home but neither was used by him. In 1910 he journeyed to South Dakota in an automobile, and when he campaigned in 1912 he used automobiles. He was photographed in a Cadillac during a Memorial Day service during the last year of his administration, as he occasionally rode in automobiles when he was entertained in other cities as a visiting dignitary. Generally speaking, Theodore Roosevelt was not an automotive President as was his successor, William Howard Taft.

The Henry Ford Museum, in addition to the brougham, has an 1891 Brewster landau in which Roosevelt rode to Columbia University to receive an honorary degree. This carriage was built for and used by Abram S. Hewett, Mayor of New York City.

Although the President never used an automobile at the White House, the Secret Service used a White steamer during the latter years of Theodore Roosevelt's Administration. It is probable that this automobile is the 1907 model H White steamer which is presently in the Powers Auto Museum, Southington, Connecticut.

[1] Hagedorn, *The Roosevelt Family of Sagamore Hill,* pp. 15, 26, 30, 32, 33.
[2] Willets, *Inside History of the White House,* p. 430.
[3] Willets, *The Inside History of the White House,* pp. 429-430.
[4] *The Spokesman,* Vol. 21, July 1905, p. 293.
[5] Accession Papers 100257, U.S. National Museum. The John C. Harvey firm of carriage builders was located in Buffalo, N.Y. in 1886. In 1892 it appears as Harvey & Wallace. From 1897 to 1904 it is listed as Harvey Carriage Co. in the Price & Lee's American Carriage Directory.
[6] *The Boston Herald,* Thurs. Feb. 2, 1928, p. 6; Same ref. Fri. Feb. 3, 1928, p. 19; *The Spokesman and Harness World,* Vol. 44, June 1928, p. 20.
[7] *The Vehicle Dealer,* Vol. 9, August 1906, p. 306.
[8] *The Blacksmith and Wheelwright,* Vol. 49-50, Oct. 1904, p. 428; *The Hub,* Vol. 45, Feb. 1904, pp. 416, 419; *The Spokesman,* Vol. 20, Jan. 25, 1904, p. 2; *The Spokesman,* Vol. 27, Dec. 1911, p. 665; *The Vehicle Dealer,* Vol. 3, p. 250. An advertisement with the following caption: "President Roosevelt Owns a Keystone Wagon Work's Vehicle" appeared in *The Vehicle Dealer,* Vol. 10, Oct. 1916 on p. 75.
[9] *Motor Guide,* Feb. 1958, p. 86.
[10] *The Ladies Home Journal,* Dec. 1903, p. 13.
[11] Colman, *White House Gossip,* p. 315; Hagedorn, *The Roosevelt Family of Sagamore Hill,* p. 166; Record Group 59, Item 92 (1902) National Archives contains telegrams and letters relating to this incident.
[12] Abbott, *The Letters of Archie Butt, Personal Aide to President Roosevelt,* p. 36.
[13] *Ibid.,* p. 359. Carmer, *Pets at the White House,* p. 59.
[14] Abbott, *The Letters of Archie Butt,* p. 21.
[15] *The Carriage Dealer's Journal,* Vol. 22, June 1910, p. 22; *Ibid.,* Vol. 22, Mar. 1911, p. 45.
[16] *The Spokesman and Harness World,* June 1933, p. 8.

Baker electric, one of four vehicles purchased by President William Howard Taft for the White House garage.
Courtesy of The Henry Ford Museum, Dearborn, Michigan

Chapter Twenty-Six

Converted the White House stables into a garage and brought in a fleet of four cars.

William H. Taft

TAFT'S ADMINISTRATION WAS the great turning point in the riding habits of American Presidents. The White House officially switched from horseflesh to motor cars. At this time a $25,000 yearly allowance was made for transportation.[1] Mr. George H. Robinson, a civilian employee in the Quartermaster Corps, was selected to become the personal chauffeur of President Taft, and the first presidential chauffeur in American history.[2]

Robinson's first assignment was to assemble a White House fleet; $12,000 had been appropriated to purchase four cars. General Bell, Chief of Staff, often referred to as "Bullpin Bell," instructed Mr. Robinson to meet the President-elect at Mr. Boardman's residence on Dupont Circle, where he was staying until after his inauguration.

Mr. Taft gave Robinson no instructions regarding automobile styles or brands. Fortunately, General Bell willingly advised the new chauffeur, and budget-wise Robinson sought the "best deals" available. He first bought a big steamer from the White Sewing Machine Company in Cleveland. A contemporary account stated that:

> The White Company, a short time ago, shipped to Washington the seven-passenger touring car recently purchased by President Taft for his personal use. There is but one feature—and that an important one—to distinguish Mr. Taft's car from any other Model "M" White steamer, namely, on either door is painted the coat-of-arms of the United States. A recent visitor to the White factory, seeing the car

129

in the paint shop, remarked: "I suppose that car has a lot of special features." "Yes," replied Rollin H. White, who was escorting the visitor: "The special features which are found in every White car. In other words, when we are making a car for the President of the United States, there is no way in which we can make it better than the car which you, or any one else, can purchase from us." [3]

Next Mr. Robinson bought two Pierce-Arrows in Buffalo, New York, and finally a Baker electric run-about car in Cleveland. The cars all arrived the day before Taft's inauguration. At that time, according to Mr. Robinson's recollections, there were only three White steamers in Washington: one was owned by a lady in the Cleveland Park Section, one by the man who ran a hotel at 6th and Pennsylvania Avenue, and the third by the White House.

It was President Taft who converted the White House stables into a garage.[4] The one-story brick structure which for many years sheltered the President's horses and carriages was then located on the south lawn of the White House below the War Department building and across from the Corcoran Art Gallery on Seventeenth Street. Most of them were disposed of toward the end of the Taft Administration. A contemporary account described it thus: "The feed bins have given place to the gasoline tank. From the pegs which formerly supported the harness, now hang inner tubes and casings. Exit the coachman, enter the chauffeur. Ring out the 'hay motor,' ring in the steam engine."[5] The task of changing the building into a garage was delegated to W.C. Sterling, a representative of the White Company. The alterations cost only a few hundred dollars. The principal addition was a gasoline tank. For the convenience of the President, the White Company established a district branch office at 1124 Connecticut Avenue, under the direction of F. I. Chichester.[6]

Prior to Taft's Administration, only carriages and horses were provided for the President. William Howard Taft set a presidential precedent by briskly riding around Washington in horseless carriages, much to the shock of many who didn't go for the mechanical monsters at all.[7]

George H. Robinson, the first private chauffeur of an American President, had been driving since 1899. His first assignment had been a test run from Washington to San Francisco in a 2-cylinder Winton which was marked "Signal" and belonged to the Quartermaster Corps. The entire trip took 45 days one way, driving every day over rough cow trails. During the entire time Mr. Robinson served as chauffeur at the White House, he never had an accident with the President's car. About the only thing that Robinson objected to as a chauffeur was wearing a uniform or anything tight around his neck. He said he wanted to wear a dress coat and the President granted him permission.

*White steamer
with winter top
owned by
President William Howard Taft
while occupying the White House.*

Courtesy of George Robinson

Driver's Certificate issued to William Howard Taft, 1913.

Courtesy of Library of Congress

Taft in his automobile, June 20, 1908.

Courtesy of Library of Congress

Mr. Robinson told the author in 1962 the story of taking President Taft to a baseball field in Washington, D.C., to throw out the first baseball. He was the first President to perform this service which has since become a tradition. When they arrived at the ball park, Mr. Robinson parked the car and a policeman told him he couldn't leave it there. President Taft ordered, "Robinson, leave that car there," and he did. The policeman, recognizing who they were, had nothing further to say. Robinson remembered that from the very first he had asked the President from whom he was to take orders. Taft replied, "Take orders only from the President," and this he did. "But one thing for sure," Robinson related, "President Taft was never a back seat driver and he'd say it was up to me how I drove."

Once Mr. Robinson made the headlines in a periodical entitled *Burgess Point Notes:* "George Robinson, the President's chauffeur, has received orders never to run his machine at a higher rate of speed than 20 miles an hour," The article continues:

> *The President likes fast riding and his chauffeur is also a lover of high speeds and has been putting the presidential car over the roads along the North Shore at a great rate.*
> *There have been no accidents to the President's car, for Robinson is an expert driver and can make high speeds without much apparent risk.*
> *But some of the friends of Mr. Taft have been uneasy about the matter and several have voiced warnings to him.*

Mr. Robinson said he could always stop the press men from taking pictures, even though you couldn't stop them from trying. The President had told Robinson that he would tell him when he wanted his picture taken, and these were the orders Robinson acted on. Whenever the President said nothing and there were cameramen around, he would simply put his foot on the valve of the steamer and let the steam come out around the car. This created a fog, and effectively foiled the photographers.

The entire White House fleet consisted of the White steamer driven by George H. Robinson, the two Pierce-Arrows, one a landaulette and the other a larger one, driven by Abe Long, the Baker electric driven by Leroy Jackson, and two motorcycle policemen, Ambrose Brown and Gene Davis.

When Taft was running for office in 1912, Robinson went to all the states driving the President in the White steamer. They went up the Mississippi River by boat carrying the car. They also carried the car by rail at times. Before President Taft left office, he transferred George Robinson back to the Quartermaster Corps.

Mr. Robinson had taught Helen Taft how to drive the electric car at her request. The Baker Victoria Phaeton (electric) was later used by Mrs. Wilson, Mrs. Harding and Mrs. Coolidge. It bears the Presidential seal on each side and is now in the Henry Ford Museum, Dearborn, Michigan.

The housekeeper at the White House during the Taft Administration, Mrs. Jaffray, was not as sure of the new vehicles as were the others. She preferred journeying to the Center Market in the horse-drawn carriages which were still kept at the White House until 1928. She refused to set foot in the automobiles, and was probably one of the few who still made use of the brougham and victoria. Mrs. Taft however, took very readily to the new transportation devices and enjoyed touring up and down Potomac Drive, greeting friends in her landaulette motor car. She was the first President's wife to ride with her husband from the Capitol to the White House following the inauguration.[8]

During President Taft's Administration, the Secret Service never rode in the car with the President but rather followed on their individual motorcycles.

The President and President-elect rode together in a closed carriage to the inauguration and were accompanied by two senators.[9] President Roosevelt had said that he desired to break the precedent of leaving together, and this he did. When Robinson offered him a ride in the White steamer, at Taft's request, Roosevelt refused, saying, "I came to the inauguration in this horse-drawn vehicle and I will leave in it." Mrs. Roosevelt did not attend the inauguration, but rather went directly from the White House to the railroad station to wait for her husband, who joined her after the ceremonies.

On some occasions, the President rode in the landaulette motor car with Mrs. Taft. This was indicated in her memoirs as follows: "Saturday, the 17th of April, the concert began, and at five o'clock Mr. Taft and I, in a small landaulette motor car, went down the driveway and took our places in the throng."

The White steamer used by President Taft while in the White House was exhibited in Boston along with a collection of 30 other antique automobiles in 1934.[10] It was acquired by Mr. George H. Waterman, Jr., of Providence, Rhode Island, and sold to Joseph K. Lilly III of West Falmouth, Massachusetts, in 1970.

In 1911 the White Company capitalized on the fact that they had furnished the official White House car by producing a similar one for public consumption designated as the "Presidential pattern." This automobile, which was technically identified as the Model M-M, was a 40-horsepower car with a 122-inch wheel base, 36 x 4 inch front tires, and 36 x 5 inch rear tires. It was furnished with either a seven-passenger Pullman body or a five-passenger touring body. The cost of the car was $4,000. A finer body could be obtained for $4,800 or $5,000 respectively. The advertisement stated that it was the type then being used by President Taft and formerly by President Roosevelt.[11] Actually it had not been used by President Roosevelt personally, but rather by the Secret Servicemen during his administration.

[1] Martin, *After the White House*, p. 385.
Ross, *An American Family—The Tafts—1678 to 1964*, p. 324.
[2] *The Vehicle Dealer*, Vol. 14-15, Mar. 1909, p. 262.
[3] *The Vehicle Dealer*, Vol. 14-15, Mar. 1909, p. 249.
[4] Roberts, *Washington, Past and Present*, p. 78.
[5] *The Vehicle Dealer*, Vol. 14-15, Mar. 1909, p. 262.
[6] *The Vehicle Dealer*, Vol. 14-15, Mar. 1909, p. 230.
[7] *Motor Trend*, "Cars of State," Sept. 1962, pp. 72-73.
[8] Lovant, *The Presidency*, p. 492.
[9] Colman, *White House Gossip*, p. 319.
Taft, *Recollections of Full Years*, p. 328.
[10] *Hobbies Magazine*, Nov. 1934, p. 57.
[11] *The Horseless Age*, 1910, Vol. 25, No. 19, p. 732.

White steamer owned by President William Howard Taft. Behind the wheel is George Robinson, the White House chauffeur.
Courtesy of George Robinson

Pierce-Arrow used by President Woodrow Wilson while occupying the White House and later purchased by him for use after his term of office. Woodrow Wilson was the first President to become a member of the AAA, having joined in 1917. The emblem is still displayed on his car.

Courtesy of the Woodrow Wilson Birthplace Foundation, Staunton, Va., and the Automobile Association of America

Chapter Twenty-Seven

**Insisted on driving
the horse-drawn victoria to church
in keeping with Herbert Hoover's wheatless,
meatless and gasless days.**

Woodrow Wilson

ALTHOUGH THE WHITE HOUSE had converted completely to automobile transportation during Taft's time, Mr. Taft and President-elect Wilson drove to the 1913 inauguration in an open barouche drawn by four horses. Two seldom-used horse-drawn vehicles—a victoria and a brougham—and a Baker electric remained at the White House when Woodrow Wilson assumed the Presidency. A favorite of Helen Taft's, the automobile became known as "Mrs. Wilson's Baker electric"; few realized that it had not been procured by Mrs. Wilson. The electric bore the Presidential coat-of-arms and was housed in the War Department garage along with four Pierce-Arrows. Three of the automobiles were built in 1915 and one was a 1916 landaulet. In 1916, the earlier models were replaced by a new limousine, a new touring car for the President and his family, and a touring car for the President's secretary. A new car bearing the initials "U.S.S.S." over the rear license tag was furnished for the Secret Service.[1] At this time consideration was given to ordering a new electric car for use by the White House. There is no evidence, however, of the purchase; the electric now in the Henry Ford Museum was used during the Taft, Wilson, Harding, and Coolidge Administrations.

The automobiles purchased in 1916 were used throughout the Wilson Administration as an example of economic austerity. To carry his example further, the President drove the victoria to church, demonstrating Herbert Hoover's "wheatless, meatless, and gasless days." He also used the victoria when his

Pierce-Arrow was sent to the shop for repair, rejecting the Secret Service Cadillac offered for his use. The Cadillac nevertheless trailed along behind the victoria in case the President should need it.[2]

The 1916 presidential Pierce-Arrow (Engine number 511-130) met the Wilsons on their return to Washington from the 1919 Paris Peace Conference in Versailles. Upon leaving office, President Wilson bought this right-hand-drive vestibule sedan from the government and used it until his death in 1924. For private use at the Wilson's residence in Washington, D.C., the Presidential seal was painted over. Through the years the beautiful cut-glass vestibule lamps over the rear doors were stolen and some of the glass smashed.[3] Some years ago, the late Edith Bolling Wilson presented the car to The Woodrow Wilson Birthplace Foundation at Staunton, Virginia, where the automobile is presently located. In 1964 the automobile was restored by Reuter's Coach Works, Bronx, N.Y.

On December 28, 1923, a group of wealthy friends presented the President with a handsome Rolls Royce as a birthday gift. The vehicle was built to order with a high top, and its wide doors bore the monogram "W.W." Orange trim on black was used to remind him of his Princeton days; on the radiator cap sat a tiny Princeton tiger. These friends also provided funds for improvements to his house and garage.[4]

Like other Presidents, Wilson had many exciting experiences in his travels. One such incident occurred shortly after his inauguration and was reported as follows:

> *He was driving at his usual moderate rate of speed along one of the New Hampshire roads when a heavy farm wagon came suddenly into view around a sharp turn. The horses, frightened at the apparition of three automobiles bearing down upon them—the president's car is always followed by the Secret Service machine and usually by another car carrying newspaper men—reared and wheeled. The hoofs of one of the horses came within a few inches of striking the rear of the president's machine, where Mr. Wilson was seated, but fortunately the accident was averted by the chauffeur's action in putting on more speed until his passengers were safely past the danger. Barring an occasional skid on a slippery road or greasy asphalt, this is probably the nearest any president has come to real danger while in an automobile.*[5]

The President loved moderate speeds as did the second Mrs. Wilson. He considered twenty-five miles an hour fast enough for anyone who wanted to see something of the country. Frequently he and Mrs. Wilson took a drive in the electric, with the Secret Service Cadillac trailing behind. A writer of the time was so impressed with the scene that he said they reminded one "of a rabbit leading a St. Bernard over the country roads."⁶

President Wilson detested the constant presence of the Secret Service, but reluctantly observed the law. He managed, however, to eliminate the motorcycle police escort used during the Taft Administration.

In addition to strict orders to War Department garage personnel regarding excessive speeding, the President issued a strict plan of operation for the garage itself. One reporter described it as more like a fire-engine house than a garage. By presidential direction the vehicles were available on three-minute telephone notice, day or night. In this way, urgent government business could be conducted even while the city slumbered.

All Presidents have been subjected to great physical and mental stress, and President Wilson was severely affected by the strain of office. Unlike many of his predecessors, the President was not a horseback rider or golfer. On doctor's orders, however, he did play some golf, take quiet walks, and a daily automobile ride.

The White House chauffeur during the Wilson Administration was Francis H. Robinson, who replaced President Taft's chauffeur, George H. Robinson. Francis Robinson's home town was Waverley, Massachusetts; he was with the White Company in Boston before coming to the White House. He was blond and tall, quiet and unassuming.⁸

A second chauffeur was Edward P. (Doc) White, who joined the White House staff during the Taft Administration and served as a back-up chauffeur and auto mechanic. Born in Washington, Mr. White was trained as an auto mechanic in the early 1900's.

During the critical illness of President Wilson he was assigned sleeping quarters near the President's bedroom on orders of the White House physician so that the latter could be alerted quickly in any emergency.

Mr. White later served as chauffeur for Presidents Harding, Coolidge and Hoover. After leaving the White House in 1933, Mr. White operated a service station at 2014 Florida Avenue, N.W. He retired to Palm Beach, Florida in July 1968 and died February 28, 1969.

As a part of the President's physical fitness program a campaign for regular horseback riding was instituted. A description of securing the saddle horse for President Wilson follows:

The matter of securing a suitable mount for the President was not easy. A horse that was safe and had a good gait at the walk, trot and canter was the type sought, and Admiral Grayson, who is

Courtesy of Library of Congress

President and Mrs. Wilson riding in the White House victoria during the "gasless days" of World War I.

an accomplished horseman, finally found the animal he wanted in Virginia in the region of Front Royal, where the federal government has for some years had one of its experimental stations for horse breeding.

The horse in question which is now known as Democrat, is six years old. He is a son of the famous thoroughbred sire Octagon, which Major August Belmont, chairman of the Jockey Club, gave to the United States government when the Front Royal station was established. Octagon was a son of the French sire Rayon d'Or.

The breeding of the dam of Democrat cannot be authenticated, but students of horse breeding would declare, judging from the quality of her son that she had some warm blood in her veins. She must have been at least half bred and perhaps three-quarter bred.

Democrat is a rich chectnut in color, with three white legs and a star, stands a trifle over 15.2½ hands, and is a perfect type of the sort of horse the United States needs for cavalry remounts.[9]

After the President's retirement his chauffeur was Leo F. Diegelmann.

[1] *Motor,* Oct. 1916, "The President's Garage," by Alan James, pp. 71-72.
[2] Smith, *When the Cheering Stopped,* pp. 147, 193.
[3] Research on this automobile was done by Mr. John Alton Brown, Sturart's Draft, Virginia.
[4] Martin, *After the White House,* p. 418.
[5] *Motor,* Oct. 1916, p. 71.
[6] *Ibid.*
[7] *American Motorist,* March 1925, "The President's Car," by A. J. Montgomery, p. 19.
[8] *Washington Post,* March 1, 1969.
[9] *The Spokesman,* Vol. 34, Dec. 1918, p. 411.

Courtesy of Library of Congress

Presidents Wilson and Harding riding to the inauguration, March 4, 1921.

1921 Lincoln Cook car used by President Warren Harding, Henry Ford, Harvey Firestone, Thomas Edison and John Burroughs on their many camping trips.
Courtesy of The Henry Ford Museum, Dearborn, Michigan

Chapter Twenty-Eight

Was the first President who
could drive an automobile and was
also the first to ride to his
inauguration in an automobile.

Warren G. Harding

THE FIRST PRESIDENT-ELECT of the United States to ride to his inauguration in an automobile was Warren G. Harding in 1921. The vehicle was a Packard Twin Six supplied by the Republican National Committee. Mrs. Wilson and Mrs. Harding rode together in a second car. This also marked the first time that a President could drive a car when he entered the office; however, the Secret Service never permitted President Harding to do so. The Locomobile which Warren Harding drove to and from his home in Marion, Ohio, while serving in the Senate was brought to the White House for use,[1] but the official White House car during his administration was a Pierce-Arrow. Following the sudden death of the President, Mrs. Harding took the Locomobile and other family possessions back to Marion.[2]

Although President Harding enjoyed the modern conveyances of the day, his father, Dr. G. T. Harding, preferred a horse and buggy, and kept his own stable. He purchased this buggy about 1915 and still had it when his son was nominated in 1920. One great attraction of this means of transportation was economy. The buggy cost Dr. Harding less than a hundred dollars, and the board bill for the horse (whose daily consumption was a dozen ears of corn and ten or twelve pounds of hay) plus shoeing and other operating expenses, cost less than fifty cents per day.[3]

Mrs. Harding's great love for horses led to a curious chain of events when, in 1923, she heard that the owner of "Clover," the oldest horse in the world,

143

Courtesy of Library of Congress

President Harding and his party standing in front of a 1923 Buick in Florida.

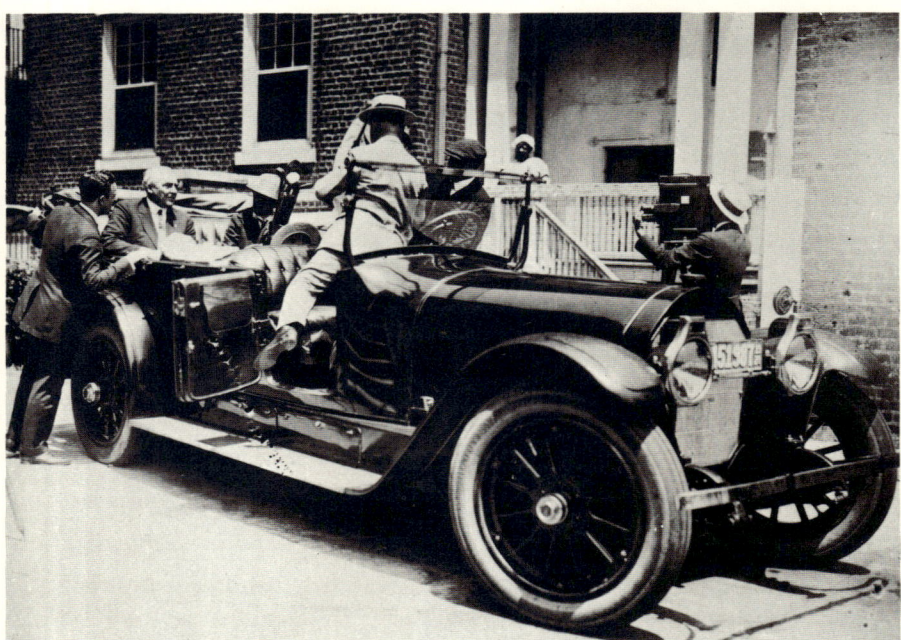

Courtesy of Library of Congress

President Harding seated in his Locomobile automobile with reporters around the car.

was in dire need. She immediately sent a check for $100 to its owner, the Reverend Uriah Myers, of Cattawissa, Pennsylvania, to ensure that the horse not suffer in its declining years. Clover lived for another year and a half after this, dying at the age of 53. The body was taken to the American Museum of Natural History in New York City. Mrs. Harding's generosity had inspired other cash gifts from all over the country to produce a welfare fund of several thousand dollars.[4]

Despite his father's fondness for the horse-and-buggy days and his wife's love for horses, Harding took to the more modern conveniences which made life easy and exciting. His leisure time was often spent on camping expeditions with his close companions Harvey Firestone, Thomas Edison, Henry Ford, and John Burroughs. The Henry Ford Museum and Greenfield Village in Dearborn, Michigan, display two camping vehicles used in these expeditions—a 1921 Lincoln Cook car and a 1921 White camp truck.

---

[1] The Locomobile Company of America had originally produced steamers, but from 1903 to 1929 manufactured gasoline automobiles. The 1920 Locomobile touring car was custom-built, carried seven passengers and its six-cylinder, T-head engine gave a top speed of about 65 mph.
[2] *American Motorist,* Mar. 1925, "The President's Car," by A. J. Montgomery, p. 46.
[3] *The Spokesman,* Vol. 36, Oct. 1920, pp. 312, 313.
[4] *The Spokesman and Harness World,* Vol. 40, May 1924, p. 25.
   The title for equine longevity, as far as this author is aware, is held by "Old Billy," a draft horse who died in England in 1822 at the age of 65. (*The Spokesman and Harness World,* Vol. 52, Sept. 1936, p. 10).

Courtesy of Library of Congress

President Warren G. Harding attending the first budget meeting during his term of office.

146 President Calvin Coolidge standing in front of his official White House car. He was presented with this new Pierce-Arrow during the summer of 1926.

Courtesy of Library of Congress

Chapter Twenty-Nine

Was a great respector of
the rules of the road and his pace was
never more than 16 miles an hour.

Calvin Coolidge

ONE OF THE EARLIEST VEHICLES which had an association with President Coolidge is a carriage made by Colonel John Coolidge, the President's father, and used to transport young Calvin from Plymouth, Vermont, to Black River Academy in Ludlow. The carriage is today in the Coolidge Homestead at Plymouth. Colonel Coolidge continued to use the horse and buggy up to the time of his death several years after his son became President.

The President's chauffeur, Francis H. Robinson, had been at the White House since the end of the Taft Administration. Under Francis Robinson, whose proper title was "Superintendent of the White House Garage," were four other drivers, as well as the maintenance and cleaning staffs. The Coolidge Administration's garage was the Army Motor Service Garage at Nineteenth and B Streets which was a two-minute ride from the front entrance of the White House. A two-man, twenty-four hour telephone connection was maintained with the White House.

During the days of President Coolidge, the White House maintained five automobiles, all Pierce-Arrows of different models.[1] The President's car bore District of Columbia license number 100. D.C. 102 was a landaulet reserved for Mrs. Coolidge's use. The President's secretary used D.C. 103. A special touring car used by the Secret Service bore D.C. license number 104. D.C. 105 was a similar car reserved for the use of the President's guests at the White House.

Courtesy of Studebaker-Packard

President Calvin Coolidge and President-elect Herbert Hoover riding to the Capitol in a Pierce-Arrow for the inauguration of 1929.

Courtesy of the Coolidge Homestead, Plymouth, Vermont

Carriage made by Col. John Coolidge, the President's father, and used to transport young Calvin from Plymouth to Black River Academy in Ludlow.

The Pierce-Arrows were rented under an arrangement similar to that of the 1960's with the Ford Motor Company. The Pierce-Arrow Company replaced older cars with new ones as often as wear and tear made it necessary.

All five cars carried radiator insignia of the American Automobile Association, silver emblems from the Auto Club of Springfield, Massachusetts, of which the President was a member. The President's car itself was dark blue, and on either side of the White House insignia was embossed an eagle holding an American flag. A large silver eagle surmounted the radiator cap thermogauge.

Outside the garage was a 220-gallon gasoline tank which was filled once a week. The five cars used a yearly total of 11,000 gallons a year, enough for over 100,000 miles of travel. Before it was accepted, the quality of each gallon was thoroughly tested.

President Coolidge had great respect for the rules of the road, but the smooth and easy-going Vermonter never had to worry about legal speed limits, for his driving pace never exceeded sixteen miles an hour. He was probably the most careful motorist of all our presidents, but he never drove himself while in office. He was a silent passenger who pondered his many problems, seldom distracting his chauffeur, while driving over the city streets. There was no fanfare about his motoring—no sirens, no honking of horns—and passersby were usually unaware of the Chief Executive's presence. The only distinctive feature of his car was the Presidential Seal; otherwise he was simply another motorist.

During a presidential cavalcade, the President's vehicle was followed by a Secret Service car and a press car. As a safety precaution, nothing but ambulances or fire engines were permitted to pass the White House car. Just as today, an advance crew of Secret Service men always examined the route before each presidential journey. During the Coolidge Administration the Director of the White House Secret Service was Richard L. Jervis, who had previously served President Harding. He sat either with the President's driver or in the car immediately behind, always ensuring the safety and convenience of the President. The President's physician usually rode in the Secret Service car.

In 1926, the White House acquired eleven new cars. Most were bought outright but one was a result of a trade-in for Coolidge's iron horse and lawn mower. The slogan of the campaign of 1928 became, "If I can't make the White House I'll take the garage."

On a visit to the Black Hills of South Dakota in the summer of 1927 President Coolidge enjoyed a daily horseback ride, which he considered strictly a "man's sport." He continued to ride in Washington, but only occasionally, and although a riding habit he wore is in the collections of the Smithsonian Institution, he was not a great devotee of this sport, and far preferred to ride in an automobile.

[1] *American Motorist,* March 1925, p. 19.
[2] *The Spokesman & Harness World,* Vol. 52, May 1936, p. 9.

Courtesy of Library of Congress

Cadillac limousine purchased for President Herbert Hoover in the fall of 1930.

First Secret Service license plates used on Hoover's convoy automobile, a Pierce-Arrow.
Courtesy of Library of Congress

Chapter Thirty

"If I can't make the White House I'll take the garage" became a campaign slogan in 1928.

Herbert Hoover

ACCORDING TO AN ACCOUNT IN HIS MEMOIRS, the first automobile owned by Herbert Hoover was a Packard.[1] In 1929 President Coolidge and President-elect Hoover rode together to the inauguration in a Pierce-Arrow bearing District of Columbia license number 101. Three special cars were assigned to the White House fleet when President Hoover assumed office. They were White House Car no. 1 used by President and Mrs. Hoover, a White House touring car used by Vice President Charles Curtis and his sister, Mrs. Ginn, a landaulet. During the Hoover Administration two Packard cars were assigned to the White House. One, Model 443, Type 315, a seven-passenger "Single Eight Sedan" limousine, served from November, 1928 to March, 1929. The second, Model 645, Type 375, a seven-passenger "Deluxe Eight Sedan" limousine was assigned to the White House from February, 1929 to June, 1931.[2]

In November, 1930 President Hoover procured a 16-cylinder Cadillac limousine as his official White House car, which he used for the remainder of his administration.

After his term of four years in the White House, President Hoover found relaxation by motoring for four months in the far West. There he traveled over eight thousand miles, revisiting friends and familiar places of his youth.[3]

---

[1] Hoover, *Memoirs, Years of Adventure 1874-1920*, p. 85.
[2] Records of Accounting and Sales Department, Studebaker-Packard Corp., South Bend, Ind.
[3] Martin, *After the White House*, p. 450.

1939 Lincoln "Sunshine Special" used by President Franklin D. Roosevelt and later by President Harry S Truman until 1950.

Courtesy of The Henry Ford Museum, Dearborn, Michigan

Chapter Thirty-One

**In 1910 he drove through his district
for his first political campaign in a bright red
Maxwell touring car nicknamed the "Red Peril."**

Franklin D. Roosevelt

LEASING AUTOMOBILES IS BY NO MEANS a contemporary innovation. In the fall of 1910 Franklin D. Roosevelt drove during his first political campaign in a bright red Maxwell touring car which was hired from a Mr. Hawkey.[1] This car was referred to as the "Red Peril."

According to sources at the Franklin D. Roosevelt Library, Hyde Park, N.Y., there was a Model T Ford at Hyde Park in the late 1920's. During the period from 1928 to 1936, Mr. Roosevelt owned a 1928 Ford roadster, a 1931 Ford, and a 1932 De Soto. The Library now owns a 1936 Ford phaeton or open touring car which President Roosevelt bought in 1936 from the Keyes Motor Sales, Inc., Poughkeepsie, New York. It remained at Hyde Park and was used as President Roosevelt's personal car until his death in 1945. Because of the President's partial disability, the car had manual controls: a lever installed on the floorboard operated by the left hand depressed first the clutch pedal and then depressed the brake pedal. On the steering column is a hand accelerator. The gear shift, however, is of standard design. It is probable that the 1928 Ford roadster was equipped in the same manner. Its design is attributed to Mr. Frederick Relyea of Highland, N.Y., then employed by Keyes Motor Sales, Inc., of Poughkeepsie.

In Miami, Florida, on February 15, 1933, Giuseppe (Joseph) Zangara, a bricklayer from Hackensack, New Jersey, attempted to assassinate President-elect Roosevelt. The bullet missed Roosevelt but struck Chicago Mayor Anton

Cermak, who died as a result of the wound. The car in which Mr. Roosevelt was riding at the time was a light blue Buick touring car owned by the Miami Police Department.

The second President Roosevelt had not always used motorized transportation. A four-wheeled carriage, known as a runabout—a favorite vehicle of Roosevelt as a young man—was sold in 1951 for $750.00. An account of the sale appeared in a newspaper, but the name and address of the purchaser were not included.[3]

The first automobile which there is a record that Mr. Roosevelt owned at Warm Springs was a Plymouth, which he had in 1936. The car had manual controls similar to those in his 1928 Ford at Hyde Park. Stone Controls, Inc., 85 Morris Avenue, Summit, New Jersey, manufactured the controls approved by President Roosevelt for installation in the Plymouth. The manufacturer had been a former patient at Warm Springs. Design of the control mechanism was credited to Marvin M. McIntyre in a letter dated June 14, 1937 from Mr. H. N. Hooper, Administrator of Georgia Warm Springs Foundation, Inc.[4]

On the President's birthday in 1940, G. Hall Roosevelt presented him with a custom-built Willys roadster upholstered in red leather. This car, also with manual controls, was delivered to Warm Springs in March, 1940. It was to be used by Fred Betts in Warm Springs when not in use by the President.

The Little White House, Warm Springs, Georgia, now has a royal blue 1938 Ford V-8 purchased in 1938 and used in Georgia by Mr. Roosevelt. The Franklin D. Roosevelt Library has a photograph of him seated in this car talking to newsmen. The license plates bore his initials. This automobile is illustrated on page 14 of *Life* magazine, dated December 5, 1938.

Mr. R. J. Englehart, Greenbelt, Maryland, owns Roosevelt's 1939 Ford Convertible 4-door sedan. In support of his claim that this car was used by President Roosevelt, Mr. Englehart possesses the original registration card and a bill of sale from a White House chauffeur. According to Mr. Englehart, only two of these cars were made, one for Mrs. Roosevelt and the other for the White House Secret Service. The car used by Mrs. Roosevelt, Mr. Englehart said, was apparently wrecked about two weeks after the President's death and was junked.

The rear doors of Mr. Englehart's car open from the center rather than the rear. The Navy Yard put a rolled out windshield in the front right. Two chrome hand rails on the tip of the back of the front seats were installed by Capitol Cadillac in Washington, D.C., after the auto was delivered to Roosevelt from the

Courtesy of the Franklin D. Roosevelt Library, Hyde Park, New York

President Franklin D. Roosevelt and his daughter, Anna, sleigh riding in 1935.

Courtesy of the Franklin D. Roosevelt Library, Hyde Park, N.Y.

Old red Maxwell used by Franklin D. Roosevelt during his campaign for New York State Senator in 1910.

Ford Motor Company. The motor contains a heavy duty generator and the car was equipped with a two-way radio. There is a hand grip on either side of the front windshield which the Secret Service men gripped as they rode on the running board. The brown leather upholstery was blackened by the time the present owner purchased the car, and was cleaned by scrubbing it with saddle soap. The center posts between the side windows are removable. The owner claims that the original tire is in the trunk. The trunk is a drop type hinged from the top. There is a radio antenna on the left side and one in the center of the windshield. The original canvas top has been replaced. These two automobiles were apparently the only ones in the White House fleet which were midnight blue in color.[5]

Two interesting sleighs were used by President Roosevelt. One sleigh—now owned by the Franklin D. Roosevelt Library—is black trimmed and upholstered in red. This "Napoleon sleigh" was supposed to have been given to Napoleon III by Alexander II of Russia. It was bought at an auction in 1872 by the President's father for $15. The other sleigh—presumably still in the Roosevelt family—is less elaborate.

A 12-cylinder Lincoln armored car, claimed to have been built for President Roosevelt, is presently on exhibit at Ghost Town, Manitou Springs, Colorado. The car fell into the hands of a Chicago Rolls Royce dealer, was purchased by the Barrack Furniture Company, Springdale, Arkansas, was then sold to someone in Texas, and was finally bought by the Ghost Town museum.

The convertible Lincoln, built for President Roosevelt and leased to the Government on December 1, 1939, is today in the Henry Ford Museum and Greenfield Village. This car was shipped around the world for the President's use in such far-flung places as Casablanca and Yalta.

Shortly after the United States entered World War II, the car was sent back to the Ford's River Rouge Plant in Dearborn, Michigan where it received an extra protective armored renovation. At this time the speedometer was turned back, which accounts for the present day reading of only 37,960 miles as displayed in the museum. Since its 1942 restyling and armoring the car is six feet longer, and it has a 160-inch wheelbase. Powered by a V-12 engine, the car weighs approximately 9,300 pounds. Its excessive weight is caused by the use of thick armor plate and inch-thick bulletproof glass. Bulletproof tires with self-sealing inner tubes, a two-way radio, a compartment for submachine guns and other firearms, a siren, and red warning lights complete the complement

1936 Ford phaeton used by President Franklin D. Roosevelt

Courtesy of the Franklin D. Roosevelt Library, Hyde Park, New York

1937 Lincoln, Model K, 4-door sedan used on the White House fleet during the administration of President Franklin D. Roosevelt.

Courtesy of Robert Hanson

of security features on the car. The inside of this black car is upholstered in brown leather.

Conflicting theories exist to explain the origin of the name "Sunshine Special" for the armored Lincoln. The Ford Motor Company advanced the following explanation:

> *No one knows exactly how the old Lincoln picked up the name of "Sunshine Special." Secret Service men say it was first called "Old 99" because of its license number. One theory is that the "Sunshine Special" tag was hung on by a magazine writer who described it in cutlines on a picture. President Roosevelt liked to ride in convertibles in fair weather, and the Lincoln was often his choice for transportation when the sun was shining. Thus, the big car was President Roosevelt's "Sunshine Special."* [6]

To ease the severe stress of his office, each president has pursued a hobby or engaged in a sport, and President Roosevelt was no exception. He especially enjoyed playing tricks on the Secret Service men. According to one Roosevelt biographer:

> *One afternoon at Hyde Park he ordered the small car which was fitted so that he could drive it, and with his secretaries, Miss LeHand and Miss Tully, started out for a ride. He headed for the woods between the residence and the Hudson River. Members of the detail were behind him in the big Secret-Service car, and behind them were State troopers in one of their automobiles. I remained at the house to answer the telephone and take care of some callers who were scheduled for the afternoon.*
>
> *When he was well into the woods the President decided to turn around and come back. He soon had his car facing the other way, but the road was narrow and the other two vehicles were temporarily stuck. Gleefully the President raced by them, and in a few minutes rolled up to the residence and called out to me: "Ed," he said, looking very serious, "I have lost the secret-service boys. I cannot find them anywhere. Do you know where they are?" I kept a straight face and went to the telephone. Calling the front gate, I left word for the boys that the President was waiting for them at the house. As I returned, the State troopers' car came around the corner on two wheels. Behind it was the secret-service car, also traveling at top speed. After telling them that he was sorry, and that he hoped they would not get lost again, the President drove off, a mischievous grin on his face.* [7]

In addition to the "Sunshine Special," a 1939 twin-six Packard armored convertible sedan, offering protection against anything up to 50-caliber machine-gun fire, was used by President Roosevelt during World War II.[8] (And before the acquisition of the "Sunshine Special," a Cadillac.) The Packard is today

*President
Franklin D. Roosevelt
standing by his
1932 twin-six Packard.*

Courtesy of Mrs. Joan Synder Parker

owned by Mr. George H. Waterman, Jr., of Providence, Rhode Island, and exhibited at the Antique Auto Museum, Larz Anderson Park, Brookline, Massachusetts. Although the cost of this automobile was not released, a similar car was purchased by a Manchurian war lord for $35,000.

The following Packard cars were furnished the White House during the Franklin Roosevelt Administration: Phaeton, sedan limousine, four touring limousines, convertible sedan, super eight touring limousine, and super LeBaron touring limousine.[9]

One of these Packards, a 1937 V-12 open touring model customed by Dietrich and used by President Roosevelt when he attended the New York World's Fair in 1939, the wedding of his son, John, and the dedication of a federal office building, was in existence as late as March 30, 1966, when it was destroyed by fire. The car was then owned by Frederic L. Duggan, Spring Lake, New Jersey.[10]

A 1938 Cadillac which was used by the Secret Service during the Franklin D. Roosevelt Administration is now owned by Mrs. Ralph G. Booze, II, Ft. Lauderdale, Florida. Originally a 16-cylinder engine, the car was later overhauled with an 8-cylinder engine. Other numbers found on the automobile at the present time are License #65 X06, engine #3134217, title #(Z) 78635 and identification #3-134-216. The automobile was purchased by the present owner from Mr. E. Charles Sharp, president of the Federal Detective Agency, Washington, D.C.

One of the most interesting cars with a Roosevelt association that has survived is the 1932 Packard touring car used by Franklin D. Roosevelt as Governor of New York. The car is presently owned by the State of New York.

A 1937 Lincoln, Model K, 4-door sedan used on the White House fleet and later acquired by Carl Dixon, Secret Service, Kansas City, is presently owned by Mr. Robert Hanson of Maryland.

Frederick Montford "Monte" Snyder, a native of Rhinebeck, New York, started driving for Roosevelt upon graduation from high school in Hyde Park in 1926. He quit in 1928 to take a two-year business school course in Poughkeepsie. In 1930, after Roosevelt became Governor of New York, Snyder went to Albany and resumed his former job of driving at a salary of $1,800 a year. He served as chauffeur until Roosevelt's death April 12, 1945.

In addition to chauffeuring for the President, Snyder served as superintendent of the White House garage for a decade, during which time he had charge of 18 cars.

Courtesy of the Franklin D. Roosevelt Library, Hyde Park, New York

1931 Plymouth phaeton used by President Franklin D. Roosevelt. Photo taken at Warm Springs, Georgia November 29, 1933.

Courtesy of Mrs. Joan Synder Parker

President Franklin D. Roosevelt leaves the White House in his 1933 Pierce-Arrow to attend church services. Photo by Acme Newspictures, Inc.

Courtesy of Mrs. Joan Snyder Parker

President Franklin D. Roosevelt, members of his family and aides making the annual pilgrimage to the Lincoln Memorial, February 12. The President is seated in his 1939 Packard. Associated Press photo.

Courtesy of Mrs. Joan Synder Parker

1933 Cadillac used by President Franklin D. Roosevelt.

President Franklin D. Roosevelt arriving in New York in his 1936 Packard prior to making a speech at the New York World's Fair in 1939. Photo by Acme Newspictures, Inc.

President Roosevelt and the President of Mexico at a meeting in Corpus Christi, Texas, June 15, 1943. U.S. Navy Photo. The President is seated in his Packard.

President Franklin D. Roosevelt and the Earl of Athlone leaving in his Packard after meeting Prime Minister Churchill, September, 1944. Signal Corps photo.

President Roosevelt's second American war plant tour, Camp Carson, Colorado, April 24, 1943. The President is seated in a Buick while he peers across the range from a high cliff to see the results of field artillery fire. U.S. Navy photo.

*1932 Packard touring car
used by Franklin D. Roosevelt
as Governor of New York.*
Courtesy of Executive Department, State of New York

Following the death of the President, Snyder became a trainee in the 84th Company at Camp Lee, Virginia.

Speaking of the chauffeur after his election on November 9th, the President remarked:

> *I don't think any of you people realize what real skill Monte uses in driving a car. He has mastered the art of driving a car through masses of people without hitting anyone, or knocking anybody down. He drove through a crowd of 110,000 in Indianapolis, and never touched a person.*
>
> *Monte moves along in the crowds an inch at a time and he managed so well that there are never more than thirty or forty people on the car as we pass through.*

Other chauffeurs who served on the White House staff, which numbered a dozen, included Francis Robinson, who had driven six Presidents and chauffeur "Boots" Miller.

President Roosevelt's lap robe and his chauffeur's overcoat are in the Smithsonian Institution's collections.

The study of back-up cars on the White House fleet is difficult since records are not as readily available as they are on the official White House cars. The following is a list of Packard cars assigned to the White House from 1928 to 1951 and compiled from records of Accounting and Sales Departments of the Studebaker Corporation:

Administration	Model	Type	Pass.	Description	Service Period
Hoover	443	315	7	Single Eight Sedan Limousine	10/28-3/29
	645	375	7	DeLuxe Eight Sedan Limousine	2/29-6/31
Roosevelt	1005	631	5	Twelve Phaeton	5/29/33-4/37
	1108	735	7	Twelve Sedan Limousine	11/29/33-4/37
	1508	1035	7	Twelve Touring Limousine	1/7/37-39
	1508	1035	7	Twelve Touring Limousine	2/26/37-39
	1508	1035	7	Twelve Touring Limousine	3/12/37-40
	1708	1235	7	Twelve Touring Limousine	1/24/39-41
	1708	1253	5	Twelve Convertible Sedan	5/26/39-6/9/47*
	1908	1450	7	Custom Super Eight Touring Limousine	12/6/40-8/46
	1908	1420	7	Custom Super LeBaron Tour Limousine	5/16/41-47
Truman	2126	1650	8	Custom Super Clipper Limousine	8/2/46-6/30/48
	2126	1650	8	Custom Super Clipper Limousine	11/19/46-6/30/48
	2226	2250	7	Custom Eight Limousine	2/24/48-6/30/51
	2226	2250	7	Custom Eight Limousine	2/27/48-12/31/51
	2406	2452	6	Patrician 400 Sedan (w/glass partition by Derham)	5/29/51

*Converted to touring by Rolson. Presented to Belcourt Museum, Newport, R.I.

[1] Jones, *Homes of the American Presidents,* p. 198. Lorant, *F.D.R.-A Pictorial Biography,* p. 44.
[2] Correspondence between the Miami Police Dept. and the author. Also, Donovan, *The Assassins,* p. 160.
[3] *New York Herald Tribune,* Nov. 10, 1951.
[4] Letter to Dr. Rexford G. Tugwell, Chicago, Ill., from Herman Kahn, Director, Roosevelt Library, Dec. 12, 1956.
[5] Interview with Mr. Englehart by the author and viewing of the car, Oct. 11, 1961.
[6] News Release from Lincoln-Mercury Division, Chester, Penn.
[7] Dows, *Franklin Roosevelt at Hyde Park,* p. 147.
[8] *Playboy,* entertainment for men, Vol. 8, Aug. 1961, "Classic Cars of the '30's," by Ken Purdy, p. 108.
[9] Accounting and Sales Records, Studebaker Corporation.
[10] *Antique Automobile* (Antique Automobile Club of America, Inc.), Vol. 30, No. 4, July-Aug. 1966, pp. 48, 62.

Acme Newspictures Inc.

Monte Snyder, the President's chauffeur, standing by the Presidential car on which is placed the hat and coat of President Franklin D. Roosevelt and the hats of his three secretaries, waiting for the President to deliver his address before Congress.

Courtesy of the Harry S Truman Library, Independence, Missouri

1949 Lincoln sedan used by President Harry S Truman and now owned by the city of Independence.

Courtesy of the Ford Motor Company, Dearborn, Michigan

1950 Lincoln "bubble-top" used by Presidents Truman, Eisenhower, and Kennedy. The transparent roof was added at the suggestion of President Eisenhower four years after the car was built.

Chapter Thirty-Two

Ordered ten new cars.
"A feature of all the cars, unlike ready-made autos,
will be headroom sufficient for the high silk hats
which are a must for state occasions."

Harry S Truman

THE FIRST CAR OWNED BY MR. TRUMAN was a 1913 Stafford. When he was stationed at Camp Doniphan, early in World War I, his car was sent there and stripped down for the use of the canteen.[1] He owned a Dodge in 1929, according to an automobile club membership card in the Truman Library, Independence, Missouri. In 1934 he was photographed in a Chrysler sedan, the automobile in which he campaigned for the Senate. An illustration of this car appeared in the *Kansas City Star* of August 12, 1934. His senatorial inspection tour of national defense industrial establishments was made in a 1941 Chrysler, now owned by Mr. J. E. Latimer of Kansas City, Missouri.

When President Truman moved into the White House in 1945 he continued to use the "Sunshine Special," which had been the official White House car since 1939. In 1950, the Ford Motor Company provided ten specially built Lincoln Cosmopolitans for the White House. These were leased to the Government for a nominal yearly sum. One of these automobiles is now owned by Mr. Latimer of Missouri. Another is owned by Mr. Milton Kronheim, of Washington, D.C., who places it at Mr. Truman's disposal when he visits there. A news release of June 1950 included some detailed descriptions of these automobiles:

> The long, low, custom-built convertible is painted black and has white sidewall tires. It has cherry-red and black genuine leather upholstery, a tan top and two comfortable folding seats. An unusual

171

feature of the car is the use of chrome fender side mouldings on the rear as well as the front fenders.

The car is equipped with special disappearing steps on each side of the rear fenders for the secret service men who guard the president. Special chrome hand grips on the rear quarter panels serve as supports for the president's guards.

The president's convertible, as well as the nine special custom-built Lincoln Cosmopolitan limousines which have been delivered to the White House in recent weeks, are all leased to the government under a contract with the Ford Motor Company, through which title remains with Ford.

The White House Lincolns were designed by Lincoln-Mercury engineers under the direction of Harold T. Youngren, vice-president of engineering of Ford Motor Company. Each car is powered by a regular high compression 152 horsepower V-type Lincoln 8-cylinder engine, and each is equipped with heavy-duty hydra-matic transmission.

Specifications of the new White House convertible include—145-inch wheelbase as compared with the 125-inch wheelbase of the standard Lincoln Cosmopolitan, 20 foot overall length instead of the 18.44 feet for Cosmopolitans, 6.53 foot overall width with two disappearing steps under the rear fenders which extend out an additional 11.1 inches, curb weight of the convertible is 6,450 lbs., as compared with 4,750 lbs. for the standard Cosmopolitan convertible, tires are 8.20 x 15 specials, a warning siren and special flashing red light replaces the conventional road lights and two fresh air heaters, one under the hood for the driver and one fitted into the trunk for passengers. The rear heater is connected to the radiator with tubes and a special fresh air inlet protrudes above the top of the rear deck.[2]

An electrically controlled glass partition separated the driver and passenger compartments. All metal fixtures in the passenger section were gold plated.

The Washington Post went into greater detail than the news release in describing these vehicles:

White House Sedan to Have Writing Desk and Vanity Case

A fleet of 10 new limousines, one of which may well be the most luxurious car in the country, is being built for the White House, with delivery of the first of them scheduled for the end of this month, it was learned yesterday.

They will have bullet proof glass. Motor, hood and sides will be heavily armored, the Associated Press reported.

The cars—nine oversized sedans and one a super-convertible are being custom-built by the Henry Motor Company, Freeport, Ill., under the direction of the Ford Motor Company, which will lease them to the government under a special arrangement by which the White House rotates cars on lease from the leading manufacturers.

A feature of all the cars, unlike ready-made autos, will be headroom sufficient for the high silk hats which are a "must" for state occasions.

The special appointments being provided, except for the high-hat

President Harry S Truman and Adlai Stevenson riding in the 1939 "Sunshine Special" White House car.

Courtesy of the Harry S Truman Library, Independence, Missouri

Courtesy of the Harry S Truman Library, Independence, Missouri

President Truman and Vice-President Barkley in the Lincoln Cosmopolitan, during the Inaugural Parade in 1949.

Courtesy of the Harry S Truman Library, Independence, Missouri

President Harry S Truman riding in an open Cadillac bearing the Presidential Flag.

room and the two extra folding seats in each car, are the idea of the Ford Motor Company and not of the White House. The company, it was learned, thought it would like to do something special for the White House.

All of the new cars will be Lincoln Cosmopolitans with standard 8-cylinder engines and hydromatic drive. However, they will have a special 145-inch wheelbase, compared to the 125-inch wheelbase of the largest ready-made Lincoln, and will weigh more than 6000 pounds, compared to the 4400 pounds of the large ready-made sedans.

The sedan being prepared specially for the President will have such additional features as a vanity case, a thermos bottle arrangement and a writing desk and pad set. It will also have special side running boards to accommodate the Secret Service men who guard the President, and side danger lights.

The convertible, similar to older ones now in use by the White House, also will have special side running boards and lights. Because of its length, a special automatic top had to be designed by the Ford engineering laboratories at Dearborn, Michigan, where all of the cars are designed.

All 10 cars will have separate radios and heaters for the front and back as well as an intercommunication system to talk to the driver. The Secret Service will install short wave radio in some of the cars.[3]

Upon delivery of the first car, The Washington Post carried the following:

Fleet Going 'High-Hat'
First of 10 Super-Special Autos for White House Arrives Here

President Truman's new super-special, custom-built, oversize Lincoln limousine—first of a fleet of 10 being built for lease—to the White House—reached Washington unheralded late yesterday under tarpaulin wraps.

The big new car, with gold plated fittings in the rear compartment, special running boards for Secret Service men and a shiny, padded leather top with sufficient headroom for high silk hats, was trucked to the Esso Capital Service Center, Standard Oil Co. Headquarters near the Capitol. There it was unveiled in the presence of a small group of lucky witnesses, moved into the big garage, and re-covered for the night.

A glimpse from a slight distance into the President's compartment showed that, while the car was not as expected, a convertible, it did have the special jump seats and luxurious fittings that had been forecast, with all of the interior hardware gold-plated, including the controls for the automatic windows on the sides and between the driver's and passenger's compartments. Separate radio and heater for both compartments was observed.

The boards along the sides for the Secret Service men who guard the President on state occasions were equipped with red running lights and special red lights were installed in the front. It gave every appearance of having the predicted 145-inch wheelbase, which compares with the 125-inch base of the largest ready-made Lincoln Cos-

> *mopolitan, and the 6000-pound weight, which is 1600 pounds heavier than its closest brethren in this class of automobiles.*
>
> *Capital Service Center attendants gave no inkling as to when the new limousine would be delivered to the White House, but it was assumed that, after inspection, it would be incorporated quickly into the President's automotive fleet. Also, it was assumed, the nine other units of the new fleet would be delivered soon.*
>
> *Rotation Rental System*
>
> *The 10 new cars, all oversize and specially equipped, were ordered custom-built at the Henry Motor Co. plant in Freeport, Ill., under the direction of the Ford Motor Co. They will be leased to the Government under a special arrangement by which the White House rotates rental of the President's official cars among the leading manufacturers. All will meet the uncommon requirement of providing headroom for high silk hats, which are essential on state occasions, and the two folding seats in the passenger compartment, plus other special conveniences, many of which were thought up by Ford engineers and designers without suggestions from the White House.*
>
> *Eight of this fleet of cars are regularly assigned to members of the presidential staff—the other two being reserved for the President and his Secret Service escort—but are available for general White House use. They are housed and maintained by White House chauffeurs. As the new cars are delivered—probably a week apart—units of the old fleet, which has been in use for 12 years, will be retired. The competing manufacturers are so eager to gain the White House prestige for their products that officials have left the impression that the rental costs are meager in relation to the commercial value of the big automobiles.* [4]

One of these ten cars, was returned to Dearborn in 1954 and equipped with a specially-built plexiglass roof, suggested by President Eisenhower who had experienced difficulties with the convertible top in bad weather. The revamped automobile—known as the "bubble-top"—was last used in the Inaugural Parade of 1961. It is now in The Henry Ford Museum, Dearborn, Michigan.

Another notable vehicle in this museum is a 1940 Chrysler Crown Imperial Phaeton that served as the official New York City parade car and in which many visiting notables, including Presidents Harry S Truman and Dwight D. Eisenhower have ridden. It was retired from service in 1960.

The Pettit's Museum of Motoring Memories, Natural Bridge, Virginia, has on exhibition a 1940 Duesenberg "S.J." convertible town car with the body made by Rollson, which was used by Harry S Truman during a Democratic mock convention kick-off parade on May 2, 1960, sponsored by Washington and Lee University at Lexington, Virginia. Mr. Truman examined it closely and was very impressed with the automobile.

During the Truman administration two custom Super Clipper limousines, two Custom Eight limousines and a Patrician 400 sedan, all Packards, were assigned to the White House.[5]

[1] Daniel, *The Man of Independence,* p. 77.
[2] News Release from the News Bureau, Lincoln-Mercury Division, Detroit, Michigan, June 12, 1950.
[3] *The Washington Post,* January 12, 1950, p. 1.
[4] *The Washington Post,* February 13, 1950, p. 1.
[5] Records of Accounting and Sales Department, Studebaker Corporation.

Courtesy of The Henry Ford Museum, Dearborn, Michigan

1940 Chrysler Crown Imperial phaeton, the official New York City parade car in which Presidents Harry S Truman and Dwight D. Eisenhower have been passengers on occasions. It was retired from service in 1960.

Courtesy of the Dwight D. Eisenhower Library, Abilene, Kansas

1942 Cadillac staff car used by President Dwight D. Eisenhower while he was a five-star general.

Chapter Thirty-Three

Had the trunk of his car broken into and a spare tire stolen during a visit in Washington, D. C. after he was President.

Dwight D. Eisenhower

SURROUNDED BY SECRET SERVICE MEN, President Eisenhower rode in a white Cadillac during his inaugural parade in 1953.

Since the so-called "bubble-top" Lincoln had just been delivered to the White House in 1950, President Eisenhower did not order a new limousine for Presidential use. At his suggestion the bubble-top was equipped with a transparent roof in 1954. In addition to the bubble-top there were 36 vehicles on the official Presidential fleet.

While Dwight D. Eisenhower was serving as General of the United States Army he used a 1942 Cadillac staff car bearing a circle of five stars on the license plate. This car has been sent to the Eisenhower Museum at Abilene, Kansas. Also at the museum is a 1914 electric car which was known as the Eisenhower honeymoon car; in it "Ike" and "Mamie" often visited Mrs. Eisenhower's parents. It was presented to the museum by her mother.

The General owned a 1964 Lincoln Continental when he visited Walter Reed Army Hospital in May, 1965. Many objects were stolen from his car when it was parked in the basement garage of Towers Apartment, in northwest Washington. One of the objects stolen from the car's trunk was the 900 x 15 spare tire. Ruben Brechbill was the General's chauffeur.[1]

[1] *The Washington Post,* May 11, 1965.

1914 electric car used by President and Mrs. Eisenhower as newlyweds.

Courtesy of Dwight D. Eisenhower Library

Courtesy of General Motors

Surrounded by Secret Service men, President Eisenhower waves from his Cadillac to the cheering spectators as he led a motorcade turning down into Constitution Avenue at the start of the colorful inaugural parade in January, 1953.

Chapter Thirty-Four

The President rode in a plush Lincoln called the Presidential Continental, while his wife rode in a Crysler Crown Imperial limousine.

John F. Kennedy

JOHN F. KENNEDY STARTED DRIVING at the age of sixteen. In 1958 when he ran for the Senate, he and Mrs. Kennedy campaigned in a 1920 Fiat touring car. This car is presently in the Auto Museum, Route 31, Princeton, Mass.

When John F. Kennedy became President, he used the 1950 Lincoln "bubble-top" which had been used by Presidents Truman and Eisenhower. The day before President Kennedy's inauguration, work started on his Presidential Continental, a plush navy blue Lincoln with a plastic top. A press release described the automobile as follows:

> The automobile replaced the 11-year-old "bubble-top" Lincoln which was used by three presidents in traveling more than 100,000 miles in the United States and abroad. Delivery of the new Presidential Continental is the culmination of four years of planning and discussion with the Secret Service.
>
> The navy blue limousine has more specially designed features and accessories than any automobile ever used for official duties at the White House.
>
> Major innovations include a series of roof combinations, a rear seat that can be raised and lowered automatically, retractable foot stands for Secret Service men, two-way radio telephones and a master control panel for power accessories.
>
> The President can ride in the car in the open air, either sitting or standing. Assuring protection in all types of weather and for various conditions, the President also can ride under a metal roof, a transparent plastic roof or a convertible top.

The car, which is more than 21 feet in overall length, is an enlongated version of the 1961 Lincoln Continental convertible. It was designed by Ford Motor Company technicians in cooperation with Hess & Eisenhardt, a custom-body firm in Cincinnati, O.[1]

The car is divided into two compartments with a power-operated, sliding-glass partition separating the driver compartment from the passengers. The rear passenger area includes two folding jump seats and a back seat that can accommodate comfortably three people.

A unique feature of the car is the power-operated back seat which can be raised to a height of 10½ inches from the floor when the rear roof section is removed. The adjustable seat, which has foot steps for maximum comfort, permits the President to be seen easily even though seated.

If the President chooses to stand during a parade he can support himself by means of a metal railing located over the mid-section of the car.

The rear seat can be illuminated with a non-glaring flood-light. Reading lights are in the rear corners of the metal roof.

Both the driver and passenger compartments have two-way radio telephones, heaters and air conditioning units.

The interior of the car is outfitted in light and dark blue leather. The passenger compartment floor is covered with mouton carpet. Two lap robes, each embroidered with the Presidential Seal, blend into the trim panel styling of the rear doors.

The car has a wide variety of roof combinations in metal, transparent plastic and convertible fabric. Combinations of each can be used interchangeably; or without any roof sections the car becomes an open air convertible.

The lightweight-metal, black formal roof comes in two sections. From the center pillar to the rear the roof has a black polished covering with a small rectangular rear window. The front section has a brushed-metal finish. When the car is transported outside the Washington area the roof is crated separately.

The transparent plastic roof has six sections, each of which is removable. A black convertible top comes in three sections. Both of these roofs can be stored in the trunk.

There are two foot stands on each side of the car which retract automatically under the car when not in use by Secret Service men. Handles are concealed in the body lines.

At the rear of the car is a Continental spare tire design which is partially recessed into the trunk lid. Two additional foot stands are built into the rear bumper. Detachable grip handles can be mounted into the trunk lid area.

Flagstaffs on each front fender are illuminated by remote-controlled spotlights at night. Two flashing red lights are recessed in front bumper guards.

Other "built-in" accessories include a radio, emergency light, a fire extinguisher, an automatic trunk lid, a first-aid kit, a siren, and special storage compartments. Power accessories are controlled by the driver who has a console unit on the dashboard with individual switches.

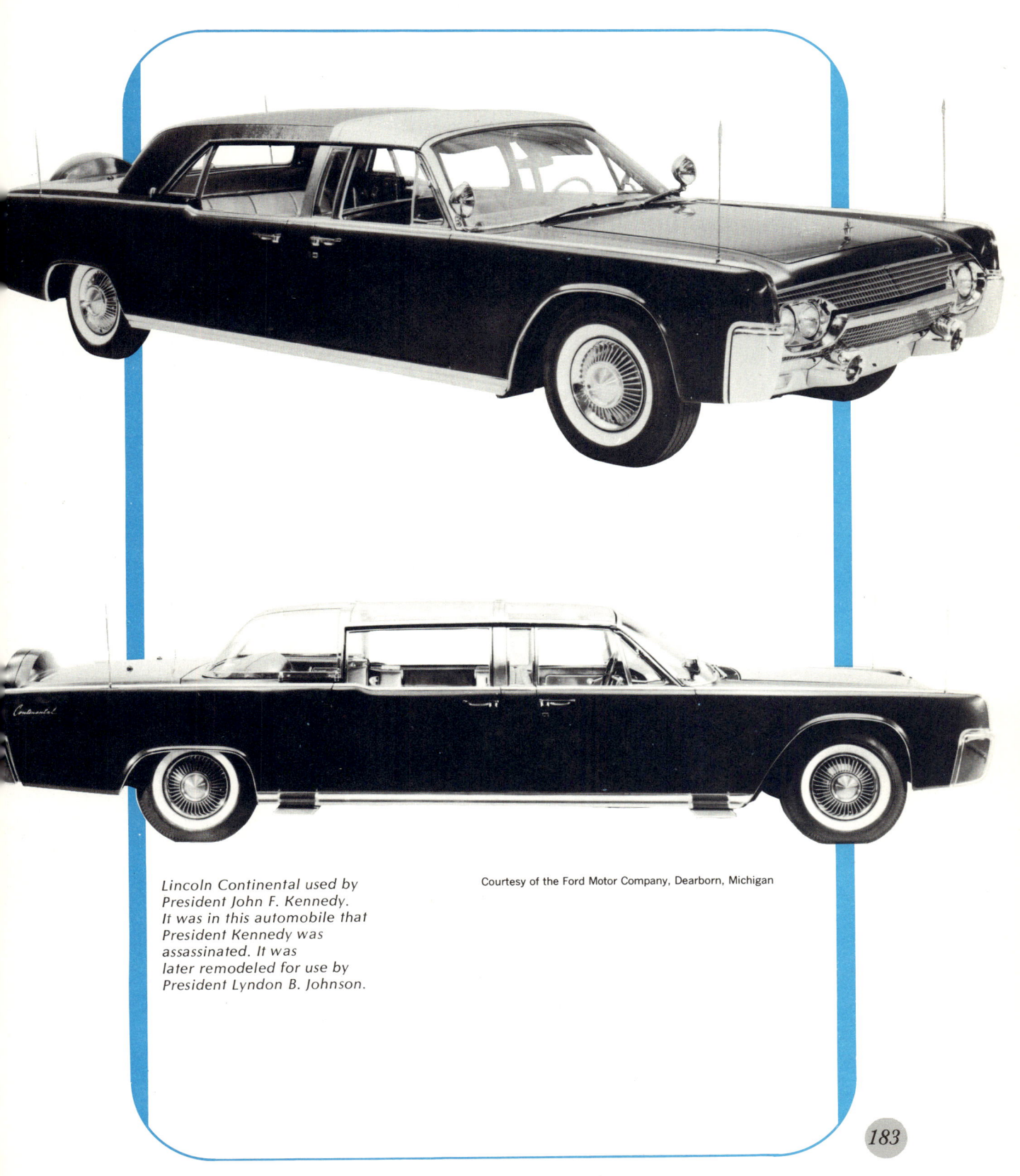

Lincoln Continental used by President John F. Kennedy. It was in this automobile that President Kennedy was assassinated. It was later remodeled for use by President Lyndon B. Johnson.

Courtesy of the Ford Motor Company, Dearborn, Michigan

*Interior of the
Lincoln Continental
used by
President John F. Kennedy
for his visit to
Dallas, Texas, November 22, 1963
when he was struck
by an assassin's bullet.*

Courtesy of the Ford Motor Company, Dearborn, Michigan

> The car is 41 inches longer and three and one-half inches higher than the 1961 Lincoln Continental model. The wheelbase is 33 inches longer.
>
> The car is powered by a standard Lincoln Continental 430-cubic-inch engine. A short turning diameter and power steering make the Presidential Continental easy to maneuver in close quarters. Heavy duty parts are used on many of the chassis components such as suspension springs. Structural supports have been strengthened considerably for durability and riding comfort on virtually any of the world's roads.
>
> The unitized body of the 1961 Lincoln Continental convertible was literally cut in half to lengthen the car to meet the required dimensions of the passengers and trunk compartments. Half-and quarter-inch steel plates were added to the full length of the rocker panels. Two floor cross members and additional steel plating were added to the front and rear side rails. The heavy dash panel required reinforced attachments at the side rails. The car is as structurally rigid at all locations as a regular production sedan and more in some areas.
>
> Special body sections were hammered out from Kirksite dies made at Hess & Eisenhardt. Special jigs were built to exact tolerances for the metal roof panels, the transparent roof sections and many other parts of the car.
>
> Drive shaft components were redesigned and reinforced. Flared aluminum brake drums were used in the front and rear. Special shafts were used for the bearings and rear axle.[2]

The car was delivered to the Ford Motor Company for final engineering tests on May 20 and in early June was shipped to the White House. Differing from the bubble-top which had a transparent section only over the rear seat, Kennedy's Presidential Continental had transparent plastic for the entire roof. It was the first presidential limousine with complete air conditioning. Under a lease arrangement the car cost $500 a year.

For Mrs. Kennedy's use, the White House leased a 1961 black Crown Imperial Ghia Limousine. This limousine took its name from the renowned Italian firm of Ghia, which added its hand craftsmanship to the standard LeBaron Imperial shipped to Genoa from Detroit at a retail price of $18,500.

The Chrysler Corporation described its Crown Imperial limousines as follows:

> The styling theme of the Imperial line has been set against a background of sweeping length. Front end appearance is distinguished by a grille of unique texture, and refinement of detail has been executed in medallions, tail lights, and other ornamentation in keeping with the quiet dignity of this custom-crafted automobile.
>
> The doors extend into the curve of the roof line and blend smoothly with its contour to add an original styling note and provide generous door openings for ease of entry and exit.

Courtesy of Chrysler Motors Corporation, New York

1961 model Crown Imperial limousine used by Mrs. John F. Kennedy while occupying the White House.

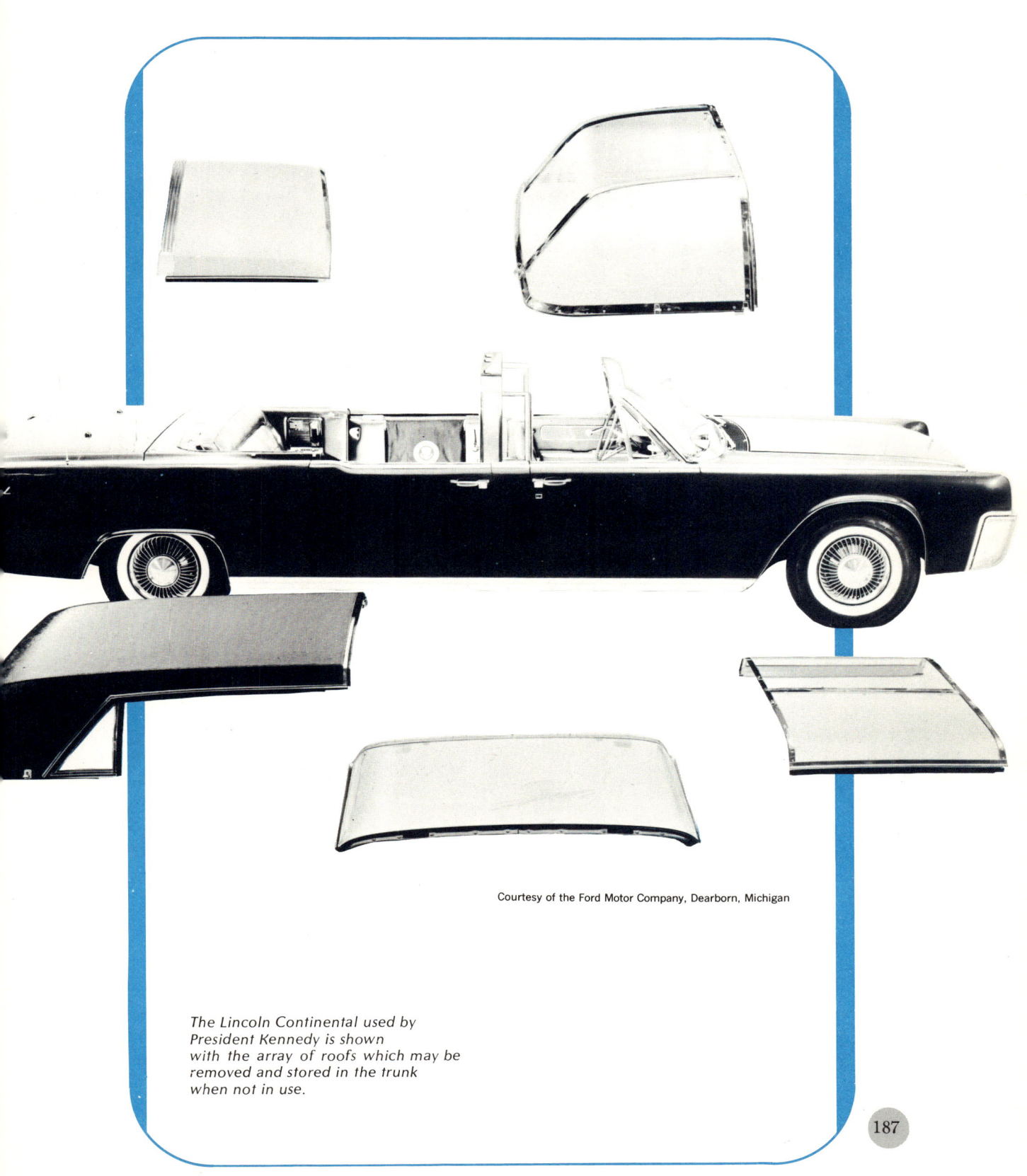

Courtesy of the Ford Motor Company, Dearborn, Michigan

The Lincoln Continental used by President Kennedy is shown with the array of roofs which may be removed and stored in the trunk when not in use.

Courtesy of the Ford Motor Company, Dearborn, Michigan

The Lincoln Continental used by President Kennedy as remodeled for President Johnson's use.

> *The distinctive stepped rear canopy is covered in black leather to match the black exterior paint on the limousine.*
>
> *Two unique designs of interior trim arrangement have been specially created for the Crown Imperial Limousine. Available in either gray or beige [in this case the limousine was furnished in a black for use by Mrs. Kennedy], the designs are executed in the finest quality broadcloth. Glove grade milled leather, cabinet woods, and tastefully styled metal mouldings are used to accent the basic design. Sheared mouton carpeting in matching gray or beige covers the passenger compartment floor. Eight-passenger seating is provided by jump seats which fold flush with the compartment partition when not in use.*
>
> *All chauffeur compartments are finished in narrow-piped black leather, and the floor is covered with fine nylon carpeting in matching black. Luggage compartments, too, are completely carpeted.*[3]

Mrs. Kennedy had always been a great lover of the sport of horseback riding and was often photographed participating in this entertainment while she was First Lady. During her tenure in the White House, Ayub Khan, the President of Pakistan, presented her with an Arabian horse.

It was in the Presidential Continental that President John F. Kennedy was seated that fateful November 22, 1963 in Dallas, Texas, when he was struck by an assassin's bullet. The automobile was flown back to Washington, D.C., where it remained until President Johnson sent it to the Ford Motor Company in Dearborn, Michigan, for a complete overhaul. Little of the original car today remains at the White House, but the pieces which were taken from the car, including the interior, have all been carefully preserved by the Ford Motor Company.

During the administration of President Kennedy the official fleet of limousines at the White House numbered 131. Because of the increasing number of such vehicles over the years, there has been no attempt on the part of the author to include all of these vehicles.

---

[1] Hess & Eisenhardt is a custom body firm which has for the past 85 years built custom vehicles for American and international dignitaries, including presidents, kings and queens. It is probably one of the nation's oldest custom car builders.

[2] Press release, technical information furnished by Lincoln-Mercury Division, Ford Motor Company, Dearborn, Michigan, 1961.

[3] Chrysler Corporation brochure on the Crown Imperial Limousine.

FBI Director J. Edgar Hoover's car used by President Lyndon B. Johnson during the time the Lincoln Continental was remodeled.

Courtesy of the State Department

Chapter Thirty-Five

"LBJ bars $525,000 expenditure
for armored cars, keeps old one."
"Kennedy Bubbletop armor-plated for LBJ."

Lyndon B. Johnson

WHEN PRESIDENT JOHNSON assumed the Office of President the official White House limousine was the Presidential Continental. Upon the recommendation of a special Presidential committee, the President decided to remodel and use the limousine left from the Kennedy Administration.

The car was remodeled by the Ford Motor Company in Dearborn, Michigan and by Hess & Eisenhardt in Cincinnati and returned to the White House in June, 1964. The automobile remained unused, as it had been since November 22, 1963, awaiting minor adjustments and a repainting job. It was first used by President Johnson on October 5, 1964, when he rode with Philippine President Diosdado Macapagal along a short parade route from the White House south lawn to 14th St., N.W., and then to Blair House. During the interval of almost a year, President Johnson had used a limousine which had been assigned to FBI Director J. Edgar Hoover. It had numerous security features such as steel plating and bullet-resistant glass.

After being rebuilt the Presidential Continental weighed more than five tons, including 1,600 pounds of steel plating. There were many modifications including bullet-deflecting glass on the top and sides and heavy armor plating. A sliding glass partition separates the driver and others in the front seat from passengers in the rear compartment, a change resulting from a recommendation offered by the Warren Commission. Previous to this, only a metal bar had existed between the front and rear. The car was equipped with a new engine and its horsepower slightly increased to compensate for the additional weight. The windows were made eight panes thick, capable of stopping almost any kind of bullet. Also added were a heavy duty transmission, a beefed-up suspension system to handle the extra weight, heavy-duty air conditioning unit, and larger bulletproof tires made of rubber-coated aluminum. The final alteration was that of the color, from navy blue to black.[1]

One month after assuming office, President Johnson reduced the official fleet of limousines available for executive office use from 131 to 20.

Mrs. Lyndon B. Johnson rolled back the wheels of progress June 25, 1964 when she rode in an open, horse-drawn carriage on Mackinac Island, Michigan, where she spent a one-day vacation.[2] Otherwise the Johnsons have stuck to the tradition of traveling in automobiles and helicopters.

Like many of his Presidential predecessors, Lyndon Johnson is very fond of horseback riding. The LBJ Ranch in Texas has, in addition a number of other horses, two Tennessee walking horses, a mare named "Lady B" and a filly named "Linda Lou." Walking horses are second only to thoroughbreds in annual registrations in this country. The horses have only three gaits—the flatfoot walk, the running walk and a joyous rocking-chair canter. They never trot and are seldom trained to jump. The prancing of the horse is the main feature. The head keeps time with the feet, ears snapping, hoofs beating a rhythm, teeth often clicking like castanets. These traits evolved through mixed strains of the thoroughbreds, Hambletonians, Morgans, Narragansett Pacers, Arabians, and saddlebreds. This breeding produces a big horse about 15½ to 16 hands high and weighing 1,200 pounds. Their colors vary from white to sorrel to black.

---

[1] *Washington Post,* May 17, 1964, p. A 12.
  Richmond Times—Dispatch, June 14, 1964, p. A 20. *Washington Post,* Oct. 6, 1964.
[2] *Washington Post,* June 26, 1964, p. C 3.

Courtesy of the White House

1961 "Stretch" Lincoln armored limousine used by Presidents Kennedy, Johnson and Nixon.

1968 "Stretch" Lincoln armored limousine used by President Richard M. Nixon.

Courtesy of the White House

Courtesy of the White House

President and Mrs. Richard M. Nixon in Ireland on their 12,000 mile European trip, October, 1970.

Chapter Thirty-Six

Was content to use the automobiles used by previous administrations at the White House.

Richard M. Nixon

RICHARD M. NIXON, during his eight years as Vice-President, rode in Cadillac limousines purchased new each year. They had no special features.

While in his New York City Presidential campaign headquarters in 1968, Mr. Nixon rode in one of two loaned 4-door, 1967 Lincoln sedans, one grey, one black, with permanent communications systems, and emergency red light equipment.

Nationally, during the 1968 campaign for major parade occasions with "open car" motorcades, Mr. Nixon rode in one of the Secret Service parade follow-up limousines. On all other occasions during the 1968 campaign, President Nixon rode in conventional Lincoln sedans obtained through Secret Service's world-wide contract with Ford Motor Company. The loaned or leased Lincoln sedans used by Mr. Nixon at all previous times were returned to the various contracting auto dealers.

President Richard M. Nixon was the ninth President to ride to his inauguration in an automobile.

The 21-foot armor-plated limousine, custom-built for President Kennedy and renovated by President Johnson was left at the White House for President Nixon's use upon his arrival. Actually, Mr. Nixon first rode in this car from the airport to Walter Reed Hospital in November, 1968, after he was elected but before he was inaugurated.

The revamped limousine features a new heavy-duty transmission and heavy-duty suspension steering, brakes, axles and tires. It also features a glass enclosure over the rear passenger compartment with a black detachable cover to provide limousine-type privacy when desired.

Besides the 1961 "Stretch" Lincoln armored limousine left by President Johnson, President Nixon also uses a 1968 "Stretch" Lincoln armored limousine and a 1967 Cadillac armored limousine.

The official White House fleet also contains two new black convertibles called "Queen Mary" and "Queen Elizabeth" and used by the Secret Service. These cars have 11-inch running boards and rear foot steps with handrails so agents can jump on and off quickly. Both are steel-lined and lightly armored.

Courtesy of The White House

1967 Cadillac armored limousine used by President Richard M. Nixon.

Chapter Thirty-Seven

White House Stables & Garages

"We read little about the White House stables, yet many incidents of interest have occurred relating to the horses and carriages of the Presidents as well as in relation to coachmen and grooms." So wrote Gilson Willets in his book, *Inside History of the White House,* published in 1908.

Prior to the erection of the White House, Presidents Washington and Adams maintained stables at their residences in New York and Philadelphia. Mrs. John Adams mentioned the stable having been at the White House in Washington in a letter to her daughter, November 25, 1800. At that time, the President's horses were housed in a stable located in the square bounded by F and G streets and 13th and 14th streets.

The stable was completed by August 11, 1800, at a cost of $1,600 and was used by the White House until President Jefferson made other provisions. In 1821, President Monroe permitted the abandoned stable building to be remodeled and used as a Lancastrian school with a Mr. S. John Thomson as teacher. In 1870, the building ceased to be used as a school and was sold to a Mr. Douglass at the price of $5,000. It was next used as a carpenter's shop. Former pupils and souvenir hunters mutilated the building and by 1886, it became uninhabitable. J. H. Small, a florist, erected a larger building on the site. The Federal-American Bank occupied the new building in 1913, and in 1924, another structure was built by the same banking concern.

In 1806, President Jefferson added a stable and cowshed on the Treasury side of the White House grounds at the same time that he built a bower-like, one-story structure on the opposite side of the White House for offices. In this way, the stable structure served to balance the office wing which was composed of a series of buildings in connected form, and which included a meat house, wine cellar, coal and wood sheds, and privies as well as an office. The carriage house was built near the stables in 1809. The foundations of these structures were unearthed by workmen during the Theodore Roosevelt renovation of the White House. During the Madison Administration, Benjamin F. Latrobe directed the building of new coachhouses.

After the fire of 1814, Colonel Samuel Lane, Commissioner for Public Buildings, made an estimate for "Extending the Colonnade Building West of the President's House 60 feet to admit of accommodation to that house of Stables, Carriage house, Granary, etc." The estimate was $8,229.06 and was made to James Hoban. To this, Hoban added another estimate for "securing the improvements and grounds north of the President's House, from injury by carriages, Horses etc. by means of a Post and Chain fence." The 1,300 feet necessary amounted to $1,040.00.

In 1819, Daniel Gantt was paid two hundred dollars on his account for digging foundation of the President's stables. He was also paid in four installments for digging the foundation for the office to the President's House.

This stable and carriage house was described in Charles Bulfinch's report to S. van Rensselaer in which he states:

> *I find that the carriage house is conveniently situated at the end, about 20 feet square. The stable for eight horses accommodates the number now kept by the family; it is airy and well ventilated.... The west wing is divided in the same manner as that on the east, and a number of cows for family use are kept here....*
>
> *These buildings have never been finished; the ceiling of the colonnades is lathed but not plastered; and it was intended to cover the whole exterior with hard stucco in imitation of stone. The appearance is certainly not in conformity with the style of the house, and is such as no gentlemen of moderate property would permit at his own residence.*
>
> *I also examined the unsightly sheds built against the enclosing wall near the Treasury office. I find that there are twelve of them and that they have been put up, by indulgence, by those clerks in that and the State Department who reside at a distance, for the purpose of sheltering their horses.*
>
> *Convenient accommodations may be had for the hay and straw by raising a part of each wing used for stables one story higher, as*

Courtesy of Library of Congress

First White House stable. 1800 White House stable at 14th & G Sts., N.W., after it had been remodelled for use as a school. It was later demolished.

Courtesy of Library of Congress

White House stable as rebuilt after 1864 fire. Shown are horses and ponies in President Grant's stable in 1869. This stable was demolished in 1871.

Interior of the 1871 White House Stable.

From The Vehicle Dealer

Courtesy of National Park Service

Stable built in 1871 during Grant's Administration, remodeled during Benjamin Harrison's Administration and demolished during Taft's Administration. Located opposite Corcoran Gallery of Art.

Photograph Courtesy of George H. Robinson

White House Stable converted to Garage in 1909. This photograph shows the 1871 stable as it was converted to a garage in 1909. It was demolished in 1911. Shown in front is President Taft's official White House fleet. Left to right: George H. Robinson in White steamer; Gene Davis, motorcycle police; Leroy Jackson in Baker electric; Ambrose Brown, motorcycle police; and Abe Long in Pierce-Arrow.

201

The President's Garage in 1916. This photograph of the President's Garage, on Nineteenth Street, N.W., below Virginia Avenue, was published in Motor Magazine, October 1916, with the caption: "The president's garage, a portion of the depot quartermaster's stables, a makeshift structure in an out-of-the-way section of Washington.

Photograph from Motor Magazine

From Motor Magazine

Interior of the President's garage, 1916, showing the President's cars.

is shown in a pencil sketch on the drawing; and this might be done, and the repair of the wings, for $2,000.

It wasn't until President Jackson's second term that the old frame stable at the end of the east wing was removed, and a stable built to accommodate ten horses was erected a hundred yards east of the old site. This met with favorable reception and the following article was published in the *National Intelligencer* regarding this change:

At the east of the President's House, about one hundred yards from the colonnade, is erected a fine stable, having a handsome picturesque appearance, calculated to accommodate about ten horses. The stable deserves particular notice, as I believe its construction to be much superior to any other that I have seen. Its plan exhibits two ranges of stalls facing each other, with a passage between; a granary and saddle room arranged in a convenient manner so that horses can be fed without entering the stalls. The floor is also ingeniously protected against rats; and there are other conveniences, which, to be properly appreciated, must be viewed.

Appropriations Act of June 30, 1834, U.S. Statute 722, provided for $6,670 for use in alterations and repairs to the President's House, flooring and terraces and erecting stables. The stable was built of brick and stone and stuccoed on the outside, plastered and white-washed on the inside. The window frame and doors were painted.

In 1857, the stables and conservatory east of the White House were removed to make room for the extension of the Treasury Building, and new stables and a conservatory were erected at the President's House under the direction of Commissioner John B. Blake and architect Edward Clark.

On the night of February 10, 1864, during the administration of President Lincoln, the White House stables caught fire and burned to the ground. The White House itself was unharmed. The brick stables had been located between the Executive Mansion and the Treasury Department.

Congress appropriated $12,000, and the job of rebuilding the stables fell to the Commissioner of Public Buildings, Benjamin B. French. Materials were salvaged from the ruins to be used in the rebuilding.

It wasn't until President Grant's first administration that the new stable was completed. It was screened from public view. An engraving of this stable appeared in *Harper's Weekly,* April 17, 1869. This stable, built on the site which was designated in 1871 for the Executive Office Building, did not serve the Executive Mansion long before it was torn down. A photograph dated July 10, 1871, shows the demolition of the first Grant stable. The new stable was to be rebuilt under the direction of architect Alfred B. Mullett.

The new stable was located on the White lot, located nearly opposite the Corcoran Gallery of Art on a line with E Street, and remained here until it was finally demolished in 1911. The stable was established in a two-story mansard-roofed building having a frame-and-glass enclosed court. Partly concealed in a grove, the stable was an improvement over previous sites and buildings. During the administration of President Benjamin Harrison, this stable was almost entirely rebuilt, the changes including the erection of a small frame cottage and workshop in the rear for the use of the employees.

It was President Taft who turned the White House stable into a garage, installing a White steamer, two Pierce-Arrows, and a Baker electric.

By 1911, all the horses, carriages—there were two left at the White House at this time—and the automobiles were transferred to new quarters. A large brick building occupying most of the square between the two wings of the original stable buildings was provided for the executive outfit. These buildings were maintained by the Quartermaster General of the Army. Even the White House cow, "Pauline," purchased by Mrs. Taft, was moved to the new quarters. Describing the incident in 1911, the *Evening Star* gives the following account:

> *Although Pauline has lost her home on the White Lot, she will continued to enjoy the daily privilege of grazing on those exclusive preserves. She is led there in a dewy morning and taken away in the twilight to spend her nights among the jumpers, chargers and draught horses of the military establishment in the less aristocratic neighborhood of 19th and B streets.*

Arrangements were then made with Captain U. S. Grant III, engineer officer temporarily in charge of public buildings and grounds, to tear down the stables earlier erected by his grandfather. The order provided for the removal of the stables from the public reservation, they being the only buildings on the large reservation south of the President's House and the State and Treasury buildings, between 15th and 17th streets. Surrounded by a grove of small but heavily foliaged trees and thick shrubbery, the stables were somewhat concealed from the general public.

The garage remained on 19th Street below Virginia Avenue until about two years ago when it was relocated in its present building.

Bibliography

Courtesy of National Archives
Demolition of White House stable built after 1864 fire under the direction of Benj. French. 1871 photo shows digging the foundation for the Executive Office Building.

Bibliography

Abbott, Lawrence F., *The Letters of Archie Butt* (New York: Doubleday, Page & Co., 1924).

Alexander, Holmes, *The American Talleyrand—The Career and Contemporaries of Martin Van Buren* (New York: Harper & Bros., 1935).

Eberlein, Harold Donaldson, "190 High Street The Home of Washington and Adams 1790-1800" *Transactions of the American Philosophical Society* (Philadelphia: The American Philosophical Society, March 1953).

Austin, E. A. & Hauser, Odell, *The Sesqui-Centennial International Exposition* (Philadelphia: Current Publications, Inc., 1929).

Beale, Marie, *Decatur House and its Inhabitants* (Washington: National Trust for Historic Publications, 1954).

Beall, Mary Stevens, *The Story of the Washington Coachee and the Powel Coach* (Washington: The Neale Publishing Co., 1908).

Baker, Ray Stannard, *Woodrow Wilson—Life and Letters* (New York: Doubleday, Doran & Co., 1931).

Beets, Edwin Morris, *Thomas Jefferson's Farm Book* (New Jersey: Princeton University Press, 1953).

Booth, Edward Townsend, *Country Life in America as Lived by Ten Presidents of the United States* (New York: Knopf, 1947).

Brant, Irving, *James Madison, The President 1809-1812* (Indianapolis: The Bobbs-Merrill Co., Inc. 1956).

Bryan, Wilhelmus Bogart, *A History of the National Capital,* 2 vols. (New York: The Macmillan Co., 1914).

Butterfield, Roger, *The American Past* (New York: Simon & Schuster, 1947).

Butt, Archibald W., *Taft and Roosevelt, the Intimate Letters of Archie Butt* 2 vols. (New York: Doubleday, Doran, 1930).

Carpenter, Francis B., *Six Months at the White House* (New York: Hurd and Houghton, 1866).

Carpenter, Frank G., *Carp's Washington* (New York: McGraw-Hill Book Co., 1960).

Clark, Allen C., *A Biographical Sketch of Thomas Law* (Washington, D.C.: Press of W. F. Roberts, 1900).

Colman, Edna M., *Seventy-Five Years of White House Gossip* (New York: Doubleday, Page & Co., 1926).

Colman, Edna M., *White House Gossip From Andrew Johnson to Calvin Coolidge* (New York: Doubleday, Page & Co., 1927).

Cresson, W. P., *James Monroe* (North Carolina: University of North Carolina Press, 1946).

Daniels, Jonathan, *The Man of Independence* (Philadelphia: J. B. Lippincott, 1950).

Davidson, Marshall B., *Life in America* (Boston: Houghton Mifflin Co., 1951).

Decatur, Stephen, *Private Affairs of George Washington* (Boston: Houghton Mifflin, 1933).

Department of Interior, *Appropriation Ledger, Civil and Diplomatic* (The National Archives, Washington, D.C.).

Donovan, Robert J., *The Assassins* (New York: Harper & Bros., 1952).

Dows, Olin, *Franklin Roosevelt at Hyde Park* (New York: American Artists Group, 1949).

Dyer, Brainerd, *Zachary Taylor* (Louisiana: State University Press, 1946).

Feis, Ruth S. B., *Mollie Garfield in the White House* (New York: Rand McNally & Co., 1963).

Fielding, Ray, *The Wills of the Presidents* (New York: Oceana Publications, 1957).

Fitzpatrick, John C., *Washington's Diaries, 1748-1799* (Boston: Houghton Mifflin, 1925).

Ford, Worthington Chauncey, *Writings of George Washington* (New York: Putnam, 1893).

Freeman, Douglas Southall, *George Washington* 7 vols. (New York: Charles Scribner, 1957)

Furman, Bess, *White House Profile* (Indianapolis: The Bobbs-Merrill Co., 1951).

General Services Administration, *Executive Office Building*, Historical Study No. 3 (Washington: General Services Administration, 1964).

Green, Constance McLaughlin, *Washington Village and Capital 1800-1878* (New Jersey: Princeton University Press, 1962).

Hagedorn, Hermann, *The Roosevelt Family of Sagamore Hill* (New York: Macmillan Co., 1954).

Hamilton, Holman, *Zachary Taylor, Soldier in the White House* 2 vols. (Indianapolis: Bobbs-Merrill, 1951).

Hamlin, Talbot, *Benjamin Henry Latrobe* (New York: Oxford University Press, 1955).

Hoover, Herbert, *Memoirs, Years of Adventure 1874-1920* (New York: Macmillan Co., 1953).

Hurd, Charles, *The White House* (New York: Harper & Brothers, 1940).

Hurja, E. Edward, *History of Presidential Inaugurations* (New York: N.Y. Democrat Pub. Corp., 1933).

Jeffries, Ona Griffin, *In and Out of the White House* (New York: W. Funk Co., 1960).

Jones, Cranston, *Homes of the American Presidents* (New York: McGraw-Hill Book Co., Inc., 1962).

Kane, Joseph Nathan, *Facts About the Presidents* (New York: The H. W. Wilson Co., 1959).

Leeming, Joseph, *The White House in Picture and Story* (New York: George W. Stewart, Publisher, 1953).
Leupp, Francis E., *Walks About Washington* (Boston: Little, Brown & Co., 1915).
Lorant, Stefan, *The Presidency* (New York: Macmillan Co., 1951).
Lorant, Stefan, *F.D.R.—A Pictorial Biography* (New York: Simon and Schuster, 1950).
Lossing, Benjamin, *The Home of Washington* (Hartford, 1870).

McHale, Francis, *President and Chief Justice—The Life and Public Services of William Howard Taft* (Philadelphia: Dorrance & Co., 1931).
Martin, Asa Earl, *After the White House* (Pennsylvania: Penns Valley Publishers, 1951).
Meade, Wm., *Old Churches, Ministers and Families of Virginia* 2 vols. (Philadelphia: J. B. Lippincott & Co., 1857).
Milhollen, Hirst D. & Kaplan, Milton, *Presidents on Parade* (New York: Macmillan Co., 1948).
Milton, George Fort, *The Age of Hate, Andrew Johnson and the Radicals* (New York: Coward-McCann, 1930).
Morgan, George, *Life of James Monroe* (Boston: Small, Maynard, 1921).
Mount Vernon Ladies' Association, *Annual Report, 1950* (Mount Vernon, Va., 1950).

Nelson, Anson and Fanny, *Memorials of Sarah Childress Polk* (New York: Anson D. F. Randolph & Co., 1892).
Nevins, Allan, *Diary of John Quincy Adams 1794-1845* (New York: Charles Scribner, 1951).
Nevins, Allan, *Grover Cleveland—A Study in Courage* (New York: Dodd, Mead & Co., 1933).
Nichols, Clifton M., *Life of Abraham Lincoln* (New York: Mast, Crowell and Kirkpatrick, 1896).
Nichols, Roy Franklin, *Franklin Pierce, Young Hickory of the Granite Hills* (Philadelphia: University of Pennsylvania Press, 1958).

Peattie, Donald Culross, *Parade With Banners* (Cleveland: The World Publishing Co.).
Pendel, Thomas F., *Thirty-Six Years in the White House* (Washington: Neale Publishing Co., 1902).
Perley-Poore, Ben, *Perley's Reminiscences of Sixty Years in the National Metropolis* (Philadelphia: Hubbard Brothers, Publ., 1886).
Powell, C. Percy, *Lincoln Day by Day* (Washington: Lincoln Sequicentennial Commission, 1960).

Randall, Ruth Painter, *Mary Lincoln* (Boston: Little, Brown & Co., 1953).
Rayback, Robert J., *Millard Fillmore, Biography of a President* (New York: Buffalo Historical Society, 1959).

Richardson, James D., *President. A Compilation of the Messages and Papers of the Presidents 1789-1897* (Washington: Government Printing Office, 1899).

Rittenhouse, Jack D., *Carriage Hundred, A Bibliography on Horse-Drawn Transportation* (Houston: Stagecoach Press, 1961).

Roberts, Chalmers M., *Washington, Past and Present* (Washington: Public Affairs Press, 1950).

Ross, Ishbel, *An American Family—The Tafts 1678-1964* (New York: The World Publishing Co., 1964).

Searight, Thomas B., *The Old Pike. A History of the National Road* (Uniontown, Pa., 1894).

Seward, William H., *Life and Public Services of John Quincy Adams* (Auburn: Derby, Miller and Company, 1851).

Singleton, Esther, *The Story of the White House* 2 vols. (New York: The McClure Co., 1907).

Smith, Don, *Peculiarities of the Presidents* (Ohio: Wilkinson Press, 1938).

Smith, Gene, *When the Cheering Stopped* (New York: William Morrow & Co., 1964).

Smith, Page, *John Adams* 2 vols. (New York: Doubleday & Co., Inc., 1962).

Studebaker Corporation, *Two Famous Carriages* (South Bend: Studebaker, 1911).

Taft, Mrs. William Howard, *Recollections of Full Years* (New York: Dodd, Mead & Co., 1915).

Treasury Department, *Auditor's Report No. 66377 and No. 66606* (The National Archives, Washington, D.C.).

United States Congress, *United States Statutes at Large 18-23 Congresses 1824-1835* multi-volume (Boston: Little, Brown & Co., 1853).

Upton, Mrs. Harriet Taylor, *Our Early Presidents, Their Wives and Children* (Boston: D. Lothrop Co., 1890).

Walker, Turnley, *Roosevelt and the Warm Springs Story* (New York: A. A. Wyn, 1953).

Washington, George, *Accounts, G. Washington with the United States, commencing June 1775, and ending June 1783, comprehending a space of 8 years* (New York: John Hutchings, 1857).

Watson, John F., *Annals of Philadelphia and Pennsylvania* 2 vols. (Philadelphia: Elijah Thomas, 1857)

Wharton, Anne Hollingworth, *Social Life in the Early Republic* (Philadelphia: J. P. Lippincott Co., 1902)

Willets, Gilson, *Inside History of the White House* (New York: The Christian Herald, 1908).

Wilson, Edith Bolling, *My Memoir* (Indianapolis: The Bobbs-Merrill Co., 1938).

Wilson, Rufus Rockwell, *Washington, the Capitol City* (London: J. B. Lippincott Co., 1901).

Wright, Louis B. & Finling, Marion, *Quebec to Carolina* (California: The Huntington Library, 1943).

Newspapers

Boston Herald, Boston, Mass.
Boston Post, Boston, Mass.
Chicago Tribune, Chicago, Ill.
Daily National Intelligencer, Washington, D.C.
Evening Star, The, Washington, D.C.
Fairbanks Daily News-Miner, Fairbanks, Alaska
Florida Times Union, Miami, Fla.
Gazette of the United States, The, Philadelphia, Pa.
Intelligencer, Washington, D.C.
Inter-Ocean, Chicago, Ill.
Kansas City Star, Kansas City, Mo.
Kansas City Times, Kansas City, Mo.
National Intelligencer, Washington, D.C.
New Era, Lancaster, Pa.
New York Herald Tribune, New York, N.Y.
New York Journal, New York, N.Y.
New York Times, The, New York, N.Y.
New York Tribune, New York, N.Y.
Richmond Times-Dispatch, Richmond, Va.
Washington Post, Washington, D.C.

Official Records

The National Archives, Washington, D.C.
    Record Group 42: "Commissioner of Public Buildings of D.C. Proceedings."
    Record Group 42: "White House Stables 116."
    Record Group 48: "The President's Stable, Rebuilding."
    Record Group 59: Records of the Department of State.
    Record Group 128: (Senate) 6th Congress, "Report of the Joint Committee Appointed on the President's Message of the 16th, etc."

Loudoun County, Virginia Court Records:
    Will Book Y

Personal Papers *Listed by Location*

Cornell University Library:
    Benjamin Latrobe Letters

Library of Congress:
    James A. Garfield Papers
    Benjamin Harrison Papers
    William Henry Harrison Papers
    Thomas Jefferson Papers
    Andrew Johnson Papers

James Monroe Papers
John Tyler Papers
Martin Van Buren Papers
George Washington Papers

Pennsylvania Historical Society:
    Penn Papers

New York Public Library:
    Benjamin Latrobe Letters

Periodicals

American Motorist (published by the American Automobile Association, Washington, D.C.).
Automobile Facts (published by Automobile Manufacturers Association, Detroit, Mich.).
The Blacksmith and Wheelwright (New York: M. T. Richardson, 1880-1921).
The Carriage Dealer's Journal (Troy, N.Y.: Journal Co. of Troy, 1910-1911).
The Carriage Monthly (1873-1961).
Carriage and Waggon Builder and American Vehicle (Philadelphia: Wood & Schermerhorn, 1911-1916).
Chilton's Motor Age (Philadelphia, 1902).
The Classic Car (official quarterly of the Classic Car Club of America, Inc.).
Coachmaker's International Journal (Philadelphia: Ware Bros., 1868-1873).
Frank Leslie's Illustrated News (New York, 1855-1922).
Gleason's Pictorial and Drawing Room Companion (Boston).
Harper's Weekly (New York).
Hobbies, a magazine for collectors (Chicago: Lightner Publishing Co.).
The Horseless Age (New York).
The Hub (New York: G. W. W. Houghton, 1872-1919).
The Hub News (New York: Trade News Publishing Co., 1891-1897).
Journal of the Illinois State Historical Society (Springfield).
Lincoln Herald (Lincoln Memorial University, Harrogate, Tenn.).
Motor Body, Paint and Trim (Philadelphia: Ware Bros. Co., 1930-1934).
Motor Guide (Washington, D.C. and New York, 1956).
Motor Trend (Los Angeles).
The New York Coach Maker's Magazine (New York: E. Stratton, 1858-1870).
Pennsylvania Magazine of History and Biography (Philadelphia: Historical Society of Pennsylvania).
Playboy, entertainment for men, "Classic Cars," by Ken Purdy (Chicago: HMH Publishing Co.).
The Spokesman and Harness World (Cincinnati: Spokesman Publishing Co., 1884).
The United States Magazine (New York: J. M. Emerson & Co.).
The Vehicle Dealer (Philadelphia: Ware Bros. Co., 1902).

Courtesy of Library of Congress

Harness Room in White House Stable during President Theodore Roosevelt's Administration. This photograph shows some of President Theodore Roosevelt's harness with his monogram and cockade. The harness is shown in a case, instead of a large harness room as was frequently found in up-to-date stables of the period.

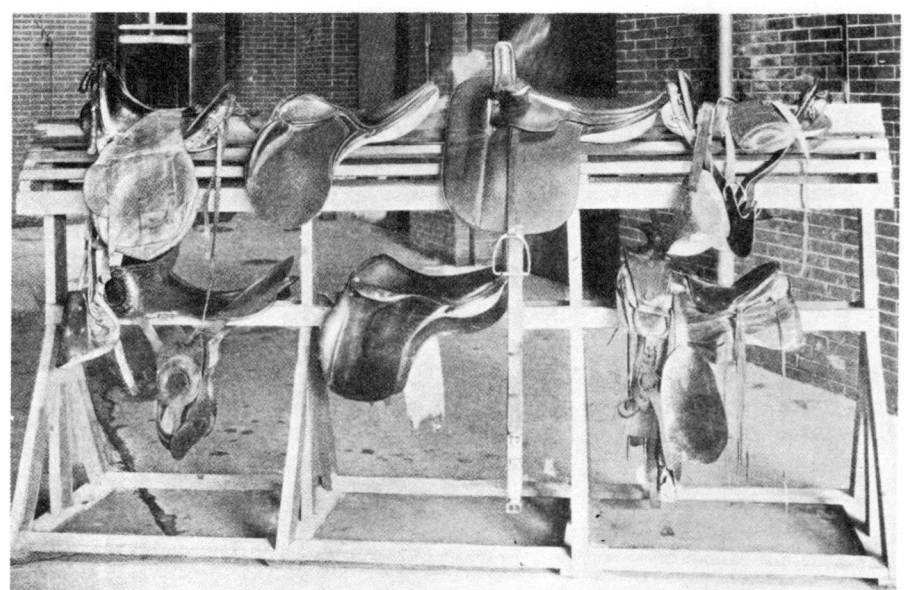

From The Vehicle Dealer

President Roosevelt's saddles. Our Washington art correspondent obtained the above view of the saddles used by President Roosevelt as they appear on their accustomed rack. President Roosevelt is an ardent horseman and, as is apparent from the saddles shown, is a good judge of saddlery ware. An inspection will show an absence of gaudiness, but thorough workmanship.

Acknowledgments

Miss Ruth Woodworth, Curator, Benjamin Harrison Home, Indianapolis, Indiana
Mr. J. Alfred Tyler, Sherwood Forest, Charles City County, Virginia
Wilfred M. Collins, Public Relations Staff, Cadillac Motor Car Division, Detroit, Michigan
Miss Elizabeth B. Drewry, Director, Franklin D. Roosevelt Library, Hyde Park, New York
Mr. Virgil L. Yarger, R.D. 1, Mansfield, Ohio
Mrs. George P. Gamble, 620 North Taylor Avenue, Kirkwood 22, Missouri
Mr. Ivan E. Whitney, Curator of Photographs, Buffalo and Erie County Historical Society, Buffalo, N.Y.
Mr. R. N. Williams II, Director, The Historical Society of Pennsylvania, Philadelphia, Pa.
Mr. John J. Fletcher, United Press International, New York, N.Y.
Mrs. Herbert McK. Smith, Woodrow Wilson Birthplace Foundation, Inc., Staunton, Virginia
Mr. Wallace O. McCaw, Superintendent, Theodore Roosevelt National Memorial Park, Medora, North Dakota
Mr. Frederick N. Cook, Supervisor of Historic Sites, Montpelier, Vermont
Mr. J. W. Moore, Custodian, President Calvin Coolidge Homestead, Plymouth, Vermont
Mr. Carl W. Sawyer, President, The Harding Memorial Association, Marion, Ohio
Mr. Hugh A. Lawing, Park Historian, Andrew Johnson National Monument, Greeneville, Tennessee
Mr. Richard Ruddell, Research and Information Department, Ford Motor Company, Dearborn, Michigan
Mr. Cecil E. Lasby, Wagon Wheels, Turkey Point, Ontario, Canada
Mrs. Robert N. Yarnall, Jr., Exhibits Administrator, The Franklin Institute, Philadelphia, Pennsylvania
Mr. Gordon Ayer, Long Island Automotive Museum, Glen Cove, Long Island, N.Y.
Miss Alice H. Applegate, Museum Curator, Aurora Historical Society, Inc., Aurora Illinois
Mr. W. A. C. Pettit, Jr., Pettit Brothers, Louisa, Virginia
Mr. W. E. Headley, Chief of Police, City of Miami, Florida
Mr. Robert J. Donovan, Chief Correspondent, *New York Herald Tribune*, N.Y.
Miss Audrey F. Haase, The Newark Museum, Newark, N.J.
Mr. David Webster, Assistant Director, the Shelburne Museum, Shelburne, Vermont
Mrs. Joye E. Jordan, Museum Administrator, Department of Archives and History, Raleigh, N.C.
Mr. D. R. Barrack, Springdale, Arkansas
Mr. Ira Glasser, Arbor Lodge State National Park, Nebraska City, Nebraska

Mr. Watt P. Marchman, Director, The Rutherford B. Hayes Library, Fremont, Ohio
Mr. Curtis Thacker, Superintendent of Monticello, Charlottesville, Va.
Mr. James C. Cooper, James A. Garfield Home, Mentor, Ohio
Miss Wilhelmina S. Harris, Adams National Historic Site, Quincy, Mass.
Mr. William E. Swigart, Jr., Swigart Museum, Huntington, Penn.
Mr. Robert Bruce Inverarity, Director, The Adirondack Museum, Blue Mountain Lake, N.Y.
Mr. Leo Kosky, Jr., Adv. & Promotion Dir., Horn's Cars of Yesterday, Sarasota, Florida
Mr. Frederick A. Chapman, Automobile Manufacturers Association, Inc., Detroit, Michigan
W. H. Bass Photo Co., Indianapolis, Indiana
Fynmore Photos, Boonville, N.Y.
Miss Jane des Grange, Director, Suffolk Museum and Carriage House, Stony Brook, L.I., N.Y.
Mr. Fred Wood, Woodstock, Vermont
Mr. Robert R. Bolton, Director, Dwight D. Eisenhower Library, Abilene, Kansas
Mrs. Joan Snyder Parker, Arlington, Virginia
Mr. J. Earl Endacott, Executive Director, Eisenhower Museum, Abilene, Kansas
Miss Helen MacLachlan, Curator, Theodore Roosevelt Association, N.Y.
Mr. Stefan Lorant, Lenox, Mass.
Mr. George H. Robinson, Midland, Virginia
Miss Martha Lindsey, Ladies' Hermitage Association, Hermitage, Tenn.
Mr. Wendell D. Garrett, The Adams Papers, Boston, Mass.
Mr. William L. Lassiter, New York State History Museum, Albany, N.Y.
Mr. John P. Roberts, President, National Museum of Transport, St. Louis, Missouri
Mr. Jay W. Johns, Charlottesville, Va.
Mr. Robert F. Nelson, Virginia Travel Council, Richmond, Va.
Mr. Grant Talbot Dean, Chicago Historical Society, Chicago, Ill.
Mr. H. J. Marshall, Lancaster, Pa.
Mr. Joseph Rotwein, Washington, D.C.
Mr. Martin L. Whitmyer, Assistant Director, Public Relations, Studebaker Corporation, South Bend, Ind.
Mr. Vincent H. Gaddis, Public Relations Department, Studebaker-Packard Corporation, South Bend, Ind.
Public Relations Department, Chrysler Corporation, Detroit, Michigan
Mr. Fearson S. Meeks, Washington, D.C.
Mrs. Margaret Frech, Suffolk Museum and Carriage House, Stony Brook, L.I., N.Y.
Mr. George A. Collins, Carbondale, Pa.
Mr. R. W. Sundmacher, Lincoln-Mercury Division of Ford, Dearborn, Michigan
Mr. Walter W. Rogers, Bridgeton, N.J.
Mr. Louis Wm. Steinwedel, Baltimore, Md.
Mrs. Margaret B. Klapthor, Associate Curator, Division of Political History, Smithsonian Institution
Donald H. Berkebile, Division of Land Transportation, Smithsonian Institution
Mr. Philip C. Brooks, Jr., Museum Specialist, Smithsonian Institution
Mr. Philip C. Brooks, Sr., Director, Harry S Truman Library, Independence, Mo.
Mr. Frank Morse, Mount Vernon Ladies' Association, Mount Vernon, Va.
United States Secret Service, Washington, D.C.
Mr. Smith Hempstone Oliver, former Curator, Division of Transportation, Smithsonian Institution

Index

From The Vehicle Dealer

White House baggage car built by Brown Auto Carriage Co., Cleveland, Ohio, 1910.

A

Abilene, Kansas 179
Adams, Abigail 31, 32, 197
Adams, John 31, 32, 197
Adams, John Quincy 32, 45, 47
Adirondacks, N.Y. 119
Adirondacks Museum 119
Africa 126
Albany, N.Y. 55, 69, 162
Albemarle County, Va. 34
Alderman Library, University of Virginia 34
Alexander II 158
Alpin, Mr. 39
American Automobile Association 34, 150
American Museum of Natural History 145
Amherst, Mass. 49
Ammen, Daniel 91
Ammen, Ulysses Grant 91
Antique Auto Museum 162
Arabian horse 189, 192
Arbor Lodge State Historical Park 104
Army Motor Service Garage 147
Arthur, Chester A. 97, 99, 101
Associated Press 124, 172
Auburn, N.Y. 56
Auto Club of Springfield, Mass. 150
Automobiles—see motor vehicles
Automobile Manufacturers Association, Inc. 117
Ayub Khan 189

B

Baltimore, Maryland 39, 48, 49
Baltimore R.R. Co. 57
Barnum and Bailey 26
Barrack Furniture Company 158
Beall, Mrs. Mary Stevens 25, 26
Bell, General "Bullpin" 129
Belmont, Major August 141
Berkebile, D. H. 27
Betts, Fred 156
Bicycle riding in the White House 95
Black Hills, South Dakota 150
Black River Academy 147
Blair House 191
Blair, Francis 55
Blake, John B. 203
Boardman, Mr. 129
Bolton, Miss Adele 25
Bolton, Rev. 24, 25
Booze, Ralph G. II 162
Boston, Mass. 20, 32, 73, 74, 134, 139
Bowling Green, Va. 33
Boyd, Major John C. 74
Brechbill, Ruben 179
Brewster & Company 95, 99, 80
Bridgeport, Conn. 91, 124
Bringhurst, Mr., coachmaker in Philadelphia 19, 20
Broadwell, Mrs. Elizabeth L. 25

Brookline, Mass. 56
Brown, Ambrose 133
Brown, John & Sons 87
Brownfield, Robert 26
Browning, Senator 83
Bryan, Mr. 47
Buchanan, James 77
Buena Vista, Battle of 66
Buffalo, N.Y. 70, 112, 113, 119, 120, 130
Buffalo and Erie County Historical Society 70, 117
Buffalo Temple of Music 117
Bulfinch, Charles 198
Bullet, Colonel 65
Bulls Neck hill 45
Burgess Point Notes 133
Burke, Edward 83
Burroughs, John 145
Burt, Nathaniel 18
Butt, Archibald 124

C

Camp Doniphan 171
Camp Lee, Va. 168
Canada 83
Canadian 87
Canton, Ohio 112, 116
Capitol Cadillac 156
Caprini, Italian artist 29
Carriages
  Baggage waggon 25
  Barouche 82, 91, 95, 97, 101, 137
  Basket surrey 120
  Berlin landau 102
  "Black Maria" 78
  Brett style 80
  Brougham 101, 103, 108, 111, 120, 127, 134, 137
  Buckboard 119
  Buggy 79, 90, 91, 102, 106, 108, 120, 123, 126, 147
  Cabriolet 111, 116
  Cart 34, 85, 90
  Catache de mode 82
  Chaise, two-wheeled 74
  Chaise 112
  Chariot 13, 14, 19, 20, 21, 25, 31, 32, 33, 38, 39, 49
  Chariot of State 74
  Clarence 69, 80
  Coach of State 23
  Coachee 26, 27, 32, 39, 40, 43
  Continental Chariot 21
  Crane Neck chariot 33
  Express wagon 119
  Germantown 78
  Gig 27, 34, 45, 55
  Jersey wagon 27
  Landau 34, 45, 91, 93, 99, 101, 103, 106, 108, 111, 112, 120, 127

Mail phaeton 108
Market wagon 32
Milburn carriage 116
Napoleon sleigh 158
One-horse shay 74
Penn coach 18, 19, 21, 22, 26, 29
Phaeton 15, 24, 33, 49, 53, 56, 91, 101, 103, 120
Pleasure wagon 43
Pony cart 119
Powel coach 24, 25, 26
Post-chaise 20
Pung sleigh 27
Riding chair 13, 33
Road coach 78
Road wagon 91, 101
Rockaway 59, 62
Sleigh 27
Spring wagon 123
State Coach 101
Sulky 49
Surrey 102, 119, 123
Victoria 55, 101, 111, 120, 134, 137
Wagon 34, 57, 90, 91, 119
White Chariot 24

Carriage makers
 Amherst, Mass. 49
 Brewster, & Co. (New York) 80, 95, 99
 Bringhurst, Mr. (Philadelphia) 19, 20
 Brown, John & Sons (Morristown, Tenn.) 87
 Cary, Robert & Co. (England) 13, 19, 20
 Clapp, Jason & Son (Pittsfield, Mass.) 73
 Clark, David & Francis (Philadelphia) 22, 23, 24, 25, 29
 Columbus Buggy Company 63
 Flandrau, A. S. & Co. (N.Y.) 102
 Geissel and Bayha (Philadelphia) 98
 Harvey, John C. & Co. (Buffalo, N.Y.) 120
 Harvie, Peter (Philadelphia) 38, 40
 Healey, W. M. & Co. (N.Y.) 103
 Hess, D. T. (Quarryville, Pa.) 77
 Jacobs, S. W. (Philadelphia) 77
 Keystone Waggon Works (Reading, Pa.) 123
 Kimball, C. P. & Co. (Chicago) 111, 112
 Kimball, C. P. & Co. (Norway, Maine) 74
 Lewis, Obed, (Springfield, Ill.) 79
 Manville, B. & Co. (New Haven, Conn.) 102
 McReynolds Sons (Washington, D.C. agent) 123
 Meeks, Samuel J. Co. (Washington, D.C. agent) 93
 Reeside, James (Wheeling, W.Va.) 47
 Studebaker Bros. (South Bend, Ind.) 80, 106, 108
 Watson, George W. (Philadelphia) 78
 Wood Brothers (N.Y. & Bridgeport, Conn.) 80, 91
 Wood, Tomlinson & Co. (N.Y.) 69

Carter, Charles 27
Cary, Robert & Co. 13, 19, 20
Casablanca 158
Cassatt, A. J. 78
Cattawissa, Pa. 145
Causten, John 46
Centennial Exposition of 1876 26
Center Market 134
Cermak, Major Anton 155
Charles III of Spain 20
Charlottesville, Va. 34
Cherry St., N.Y. 20
Chauffeurs
 Brechbill, Ruben 179
 Jackson, Leroy 133
 Long, Abe 133
 Robinson, Francis H. 139, 147, 168
 Robinson, George H. 129, 130, 133, 134, 139
 Snyder, Frederick Montford "Monte" 162, 168
 White, Edward P. "Doc" 139
Cheshire, Conn. 27
Chesterbrook Farms, Berwyn 78
Chicago Historical Society 82
Chicago, Ill. 82, 111, 112, 120
Chicago Inter-Ocean 63
Chicago Rolls Royce dealer 158
Chicago World's Fair, 1893 80
Chichester, F.I. 130
Chrysler Corporation 185
Cincinnati, Ohio 53, 57, 182, 191
Clark, David & Francis 22, 23, 24, 25, 29
Clark, Edward 203
Clapp, Jason & Son 73
Cleveland, Grover 101, 103, 104, 106, 111, 116
Cleveland, Mrs. Grover 101, 103
Cleveland, Ohio 98, 129, 130
Cleveland Park Section 130
Coachmakers—see carriage makers

Coachmen
 Burke, Edward (Canadian) 83
 Fagan, John (Hessian) 25
 Gaceer, John "Dutch John" or "Fritz" (German) 27
 Giles, John 78
 Hawkins, Albert (Negro) 91, 97, 101, 103, 108
 Henry 75
 Leary, Jeremy 46
 Lee, Charlie (Negro) 91
 Lemos, Beverly 103
 McGee, Patterson 83
 Seaman 119
 Tom (Negro) 120

Coats, William 15
Columbian Exposition of 1893 63
Columbia Commandery of Knights Templar 97
Columbia University 127
Columbus Buggy Company 63
Committee for the Re-enactment of Lincoln's Inauguration 93
Concord, N.H. 74, 75
Conkling, Roscoe 89
Conrad and McMunn, Messrs. 34
"Constitution" 48, 49
Continental Congress 15
Cooke, A. B. W. 25
Coolidge, Calvin 137, 139, 147, 150, 153
Coolidge, Colonel John 147
Coolidge Homestead 147
Coolidge, Mrs. Calvin 120, 147
Cooper, (hackman) 83
Corcoran Art Gallery 130, 204
Cortelyou, Secretary 124
Cowles, Captain 123
Craig, Big Bill 124
Crane, Governor Murray 124
Crosby, William C. 27
Culpeper, Va. 27
Cumberland, Maryland 66
Cunningham, Mrs. A. W. 82
Curtin, Richard 91
Curtis, Vice President Charles 153
Custis, G. W. P. 24, 29
Custis, Martha Dandridge 13
Cutts, Mr. 40

D

Daily National Intelligencer 85
Dallas, Texas 189
Dalzell Axle Co. 113
Danville, Va. 27
Davidson, William 25
Davis, Gene 133
Davis, Zib 116
Dearborn, Michigan 120, 134, 145, 175, 176, 189
Decatur, Mr. 21, 26
Declaration of Independence 34
Democratic friends of Boston 73
Democratic-Republican 49
DeNaige, Mr. 124
Dickenson, General 19
Dietrich Co. 162
Dimmick, Mrs. 108
Diverson, Thomas 33
Dixon, Carl 162
Dixon, Senator James 86
Doherty Ranch, Texas 126
Donelsons of "Tulip Grove," Hermitage, Tenn. 47
Douglass, Mr. 197
Drawing Room Companion 25
Duggan, Frederic L. 162
Dunbar, Colonel Peter 74
Duryea, Frank 116
Dunlap, Mrs. Mary 29
Dutch John 27
Dutch Reformed Church 56
Dwight D. Eisenhower Museum 179

E

Eaton, John H. 47
Eaton, Mrs. Lillie 108
Eberlein, Mr. 21
Edison, Thomas 145
Eisenhower, Dwight D. 176, 179, 181
Eisenhower, Mrs. Dwight D. 179
Elzey, Dr. 33
England 15, 124
Englehart, R. J. 156
Eppes, Jack 34
Esso Capital Service Center 175, 176
Executive Mansion 34, 41, 82, 203
Executive Office Building 203

F

Fairfax Co., Va. 24
Fagan, John 25
Franklin Institute 19
The Federal-American Bank 197
F.B.I. Director 191
Federal Detective Agency 162
Fredericksburg, Va. 13, 44
Ferris, J. L. G. 19
Fillmore, Millard 69, 70
Fillmore, Mrs. Millard 69, 70
Finley, Mr. 39
Fire of 1814 198
Firestone, Harvey 145
Flandrau, A. S. & Co. 102

Folsom, Frances 101
Footman
    Causten, John 46
    Forbes, Charles (Ireland) 83
Ford, Henry 145
Ford Motor Company 150, 158, 160, 171, 176, 182, 185, 189, 191, 195
Ford's River Rouge Plant 158
Ford's Theatre 80
Ft. Lauderdale, Fla. 162
France 33
Franklin D. Roosevelt Library 155, 156, 158
Frederick of Prussia 29
Freeport, Ill. 172, 176
Fremont, Ohio 95
French, Benjamin B. 203
Front Royal, Va. 141
"Fritz" 27

G

Gaceer, John 27
Galveston, Texas 126
Gamble, Mrs. George Peterkin 62
Garfield, James A. 95, 97, 98, 101
Geissel and Bayha 98
General of the U.S. Army 179
Genoa 185
Georgetown, D.C. 41, 83
Georgetown Heights 91
George Washington Bicentennial 93
Georgia Warm Springs Foundation Inc. 156
Germantown, Pa. 19
Ghost Town, Colo. 158
Giles, John 78
Giles, Mr. 25
Ginn, Mrs. 153
Goshen, Ind. 120
Grant, Capt. U.S. III 204
Grant, Gen. Frederick Dent 90, 93
Grant, Mrs. U. S. 93
Grant, U. S. 89, 90, 91, 93, 101, 203
    Tour around the world 93
Grayson, Admiral 139
Greenbelt, Md. 156
Greeneville, Tenn. 85
Grimsley, Elizabeth Todd 80
Guiteau, Charles J. 98
Gwynn, Dr. 48

H

Hackensack, N.J. 155
Hackman at White House
    Cooper 83
Halford, Secretary 108
Hall of Congress 19
Hall, Frank 119
Halsey & Smith 113
Hambletonian colt 90, 192
Hannaford, F. W. 74
Hanse, Conrad 33, 37
Hanson, Robert 162
Harding, Dr. G. T. 143
Harding, Mrs. Warren G. 143, 145
Harding, Warren G. 116, 137, 139, 143, 145, 150

Harper's Weekly 203
Harrison, Benjamin 103, 106, 108, 204
Harrison, Mrs. Benjamin 108
Harrison, William Henry 57
Hartford, Conn. 86
Harvard 124
Harvie, Peter, 38, 40
Hawkins, Albert (coachman) 91, 97, 101, 109
Hayes, C. L. 108
Hayes, Rutherford B. 95, 97, 101
Hayes, Webb 95
Harry S Truman Library 171
Harvey, John C. & Co. 120
Healey, W. M. & Co. 103
Henry, (coachman) 75
Henry Motor Company 176
The Henry Ford Museum and Greenfield Village
   27, 120, 127, 134, 137, 145, 158, 176
Herbert, Mr. 27
The Hermitage 48, 49, 53
Hess, D. T. 77
Hess & Eisenhardt 182, 191
Hessian coachman 25
Hewett, Abram S. 127
Highland, N.Y. 155
Hoes, Laurence G. 44
Hofheins, Edward A. 123
Hoomes, Colonel John 33
Hooper, H. N. 156
Hoover, Herbert 137, 139, 153
Hoover, J. Edgar 191
Hoover, Mrs. Herbert 153
Horses, ponies, etc.
  Abdullah 108
  Algonquin 124
  Audrey 124
  Bassett M. 120
  Billy 108
  Billy Button 90
  Billy H. 120
  Billy T. 120
  Bleistein 124
  Blueskin 18
  Bob 58
  Butcher Boy 90
  Caesar 31
  Caution 119
  Charley 58
  Cleopatra 31
  Cincinnatus 90
  Clover 143, 145
  Cuba 119
  Democrat 141
  Diamond 119
  Egypt 90
  Exem, Prince 120
  Exem, Tom 120
  General Grant 119
  Georgia 124
  Golden Farmer 74
  Greenbrier 120
  Grey Dawn 124
  Jacko Root 124
  Jennie 90
  John 58, 108
  Julia 90
  Hawpatch 120
  Knight of Malta 21
  Lady B. 192
  Larry 124
  Leopard 93
  Lexington 108
  Linda Lou 192
  Linden Tree 93
  Magna Carta 120
  Magnolia 18
  Mary 90
  Mike 58
  Nelson, 18, 20
  Octagon 141
  Old Whitey 66
  Oward 120
  Pickle 119
  Rayon d'Or 141
  Reb 90
  Renown 124
  Rosewell 124
  Royal Gift 21
  Rusty 124
  Sagamore 119
  St. Louis 90
  Texas 119
  Toby 58
  Truxton 53
  Union 75
  Wildair 33
  Wyoming 124
  Yagenka 124
Hudson River 160
Hunter, Robert (London merchant) 18
Hurley, James (postilion) 25
Hyde Park, N.Y. 155, 156, 160, 162

I

Illinois 83
Inaugurations 1789, 20; 1793, 19; 1801, 33, 34;
  1805, 34; 1809, 37, 38; 1821, 43; 1825, 45;
  1829, 47; 1833, 47; 1837, 53; 1841, 57;
  1845, 63; 1849, 65, 66; 1853, 73; 1861, 80;
  1873, 93; 1877, 95; 1881, 97; 1885, 101;
  1889, 103; 1897, 104, 111; 1909, 134; 1913,
  137; 1921, 143; 1929, 153; 1953, 179
Indianapolis, Ind. 108, 168
Ireland 83
Irving Hotel 66
Irwin, Robert 79

J

Jackson, Andrew 47, 48, 49, 53, 86, 203
Jackson, Colonel 53
Jackson, Leroy 133
Jackson, Major 25
Jackson, Sarah Y. 48
Jacobs, S. W. 77
Jaffray, Mrs. Elizabeth 120, 134
James A. Garfield home 98
James Buchanan Foundation 78
Jefferson, Thomas 25, 32, 33, 34, 37, 38, 197, 198
Jervis, Richard L. 150
Johnson, Andrew 85, 86
Johnson, Eliza 85
Johnson, Lyndon B. 191, 192
Johnson, Mrs. L. B. 192
Johnson, Walter 27
Jones and Kain 34

Jones, Ball & Co. 74
Jones, Joseph 15
Jones, Senator John P. 89
Jordon, N.Y. 74
J. Sterling Morton Monument 104

K

Kansas City, Mo. 162, 171
Kansas City Star 171
Kellogg, Frank 124
Kennedy, Captain Archibald 19
Kennedy, John F. 181, 182, 185, 189, 191, 195
Kennedy, Mrs. John F. 181, 185, 189
Kentucky 79
Kettletass, Peter 20
Keyes Motor Sales Inc. 155
Keystone Wagon Works 123
Kimbal, C. P. & Co. 74, 111, 112
Kirksite dies 185
Knox, Henry 25
Kopcsay, Joseph 108
Kronheim, Milton 171
Krout, Mary H. 63

L

Ladies Hermitage Association 48
Lafayette, General 21, 55
Laird, Mrs. Eleanor Cassatt 78
Lake County Historical Society 98
Lamont, Daniel 103
Lancaster, Pa. 15
Lancastrian School 197
Lane, Colonel Samuel 198
Lane, Harriet 77, 78
Larz Anderson Park, Brookline, Mass. 162
La Salle County Historical Museum 83
Lasby, Cecil E. 116
Latimer, J. E. 171
Latrobe, Benjamin F. 38, 40, 198
Law, Thomas 34
Lawrence, Mrs. Rachael Jackson 48
L. B. J. Ranch 192
Lear, Tobias 20, 21, 23
Leary, Jeremy 46
Lee, Charlie (coachman) 91
Lee, Grandfather 119
Le Hand, Miss 160
Le Havre 33
Lemos, Beverly (coachman) 103
Leschot, Lewis A. 34
Lewis, Betty Washington 27
Lewis, Fielding 13
Lewis, George 15
Lewis, Obed 79
Lexington, Va. 176
Lincoln, Abraham 65, 79, 80, 82, 82, 86, 203
Lincoln-Douglas Debate 83
Lincoln, Mary Todd 80, 82
Lincoln-Mercury engineers 172
Lincoln, Robert Todd 83, 85
Lincoln, Tad 82
Little White House 156
Locomobile Co. 116
Loeb, Secretary 120

London, England 18, 39, 45, 55, 56
Long, Abe 133
Loring, Caleb G. & Co. 74
Louis XVI of France 19
Low, Mess. 86
Ludlow 147
Ludlow, Israel L. 57
Ludwig, John 27
Ludwig, Molly 27

M

McAllaster, Charles 57
McGee, Patterson 83
McGrann, Richard 78
McIntyre, Marvin M. 156
McKee, Mrs. 108
McKinley, Mrs. William 112, 113, 116
McKinley, William 111, 112, 113, 116, 119
McReynolds Sons 123
Macapagal, Diosdado (President, Philippines) 191
Mackinac Island, Mich. 192
Madison, James 37, 38, 198
Madison, Mrs. James (Dolley) 38, 39, 40, 41
Manchurian war lord 162
Manhattan Island, N.Y. 20
Manitou Springs, Colo. 158
Manly, Robert 21
Mansfield, Ohio 98
Manville, B. & Co. 102
Marion, Ohio 143
Marshall, Henry J. 78
Maryland 65, 162
Marvin, Legrand 86
Mason, George 27
Mauld, John (Washington's valet) 25
Meadow Mountain 65
Meade, Bishop of Virginia 24
Meeks, Fearson S. 93
Meeks, Samuel J. Company 93
Melville Collection 77
Memorial Day 126
Menton, Ohio 98
Mexican saddle 75
Mexico 66
Miami, Fla. 155
Miami Police Department 156
Milburn home 116
Miller, "Boots" (chauffeur) 168
Mississippi River 133
Mitchell, John 19, 20
Monroe, James 43, 44, 197
  Tour of the Northern States 43
Monterey, Battle of 66
Monticello 33, 34, 37
Montpelier 39
Morgan, Edward (White House attendant) 69
Morgans 192
Morris House 21
Morristown, Tenn. 87
Motor vehicles
  Baker electric 130, 133, 134, 137, 204
  "Bubble Top" 176, 179, 181
  Buick touring car 156
  Cadillac 126, 138, 153, 160, 162, 179, 195
  Chrysler 171
  Chrysler Crown Imperial Phaeton 176
  Crown Imperial Ghia limousine 185, 189

Deluxe Eight Sedan limousine 153
De Sota 155
Duesenberg 176
Eisenhower "honeymoon car" 179
Ford 155, 156
Ford phaeton 155
Ford roadster 155
Horseless buggy 116
Landaulet or landaulett 133, 134, 137, 147, 153
LeBaron Imperial 185
LeBaron touring car 162
Lincoln 158, 160, 162, 179, 182, 195, 196
Lincoln Continental 182, 185
Lincoln Cook car 145
Lincoln Cosmopolitan 171, 172, 175, 181
Locomobile 116, 143
Maxwell touring car 155
Model "T" Ford 155
Motorcycle 133
"Old 99" 160
Packard 153, 160, 162, 168, 177
Packard Twin Six 143
Pierce-Arrow 133, 137, 143, 147, 150, 153, 204
Plymouth 156
Presidential Continental 181, 185, 189, 191
"Queen Elizabeth" 196
"Queen Mary" 196
"Red Peril" 155
Rolls Royce 138
Single Eight Sedan limousine 153
"Sunshine Special" 160, 171
Stafford 171
White camp truck 145
White steamer 127, 130, 133, 134, 204
Willys roadster 156
Winton 130
Mount Vernon, Va. 15, 18, 20, 24, 25, 26
Michigan Vice-Regent 26
Mullett, Alfred B. 203
Myers, Reverend Uriah 145

N

Napoleon III 158
Narragansett Prancers 192
Nashville, Tenn. 49
National Horse Show Association 80
National Intelligencer 34, 203
Natural Bridge, Va. 176
Navy Yard 156
Nebraska City, Neb. 104
Newark, N.J. 113
New Hampshire 100, 138
New Haven, Conn. 102
New Mexico 126
New Orleans, La. 65
New York City 18, 20, 21, 49, 56, 63, 69, 70, 74, 80, 85, 86, 91, 93, 95, 97, 99, 102, 103, 113, 127, 145, 176, 195, 197
New York bankers 85
New York Merchants group 80
New York State 162
    Governor of 162
New York Times 27
New York World's Fair, 1939 56, 162

Newrich, Mr. 57
Nicholas, (horse caretaker) 87
Nicolay, John 82
Nixon, Richard M. 195, 196
Norfolk County, Mass. 46
North Bend, Ohio 57, 108
Norway, Me. 74

O

Oak Hill 43, 44
Oak Hill Cemetery 83
Oak View 101
Ohio River 65
Oklahoma 126
"Old Ironsides" 53
Old Hickory 49
Old Pike 65
Osborne, William 25
Ottawa, Ill. 83
Oyster Bay, N.Y. 124

P

Page, Mr. 26
Pakistan, President of 189
Palm Beach, Fla. 139
Palo Alto, Battle of 66
Pan-American Exposition 116
Paris, Mr. 25
Paris Peace Conference, 1919 138
Paulding coat-of-arms 59
Paulding, Secretary of Navy 59
"Pauline" (White House cow) 204
Peace Treaty, 1815 45
Pelham, N.Y. 25
Penn, Richard 15, 22
Pennsylvania, Governor of 15, 19
Pennsylvania, State of 15, 19
Pennsylvania Ave., Washington, D.C. 37, 47, 53, 57, 66, 130
Petit, Mr. 20
Pettit's Museum of Motoring Memories 176
Pierce-Arrow Company 150
Pitcher, Molly 27
Philadelphia, Pa. 15, 18, 20, 21, 22, 23, 25, 26, 29, 31, 38, 39, 40, 43, 48, 57, 77, 78, 98, 197
Philadelphia, Mayor of 24
Pierce, Franklin 73, 74
Pittsfield, Mass. 73, 124
Plymouth, Vt. 147
"Pocahontas" (Tyler's boat) 62
Polk, James K. 63, 64, 66
Pontoosuc Company 73
Potomac Drive 134
Poughkeepsie, N.Y. 27, 155
Powel, Elizabeth 25, 26
Powel family 25
Powel, John Ham 25
Powel, Mrs. Samuel 24
Powers Auto Museum 127
President's House 198, 203
Presidential Mansion 31
Presidential Seal 182

Princeton, N.J. 27, 104
Princeton University 138
Providence, R.I. 134, 162

Q

Quarryville, Pa. 77
Quartermaster Corps 120, 129, 133
Quartermaster's Department 126
Quartermaster General of the Army 204
Quincy coat-of-arms 31
Quincy, Mass 32, 46
Quidada, Jose 126

R

Randolph, Thomas Jefferson IV 34
Raymond, Henry J. 65
Reading, Pa. 123
Red Bank, N.J. 27
Red Top 101
Reeside, James 47
Reeves, Christopher 14
Reibelt, J. P. 34
Relyea, Frederick 155
Renaudet, Peter (Philadelphia physician) 15
Republican National Committee 143
Resaca de la Palma, Battle of 66
Riley, Miss 120
Rittenhouse, David 15
Robinson, Francis H. 139, 147, 168
Robinson, George H. 129, 130, 133, 134, 139
Rollson 176
Rome, Italy 29
Roosevelt, Ethel 123
Roosevelt, Franklin D. 155, 156, 158, 162, 168
Roosevelt, John 162
Roosevelt, G. Hall 156
Roosevelt, Mrs. Edith 119
Roosevelt, Mrs. F. D. 156
Roosevelt, Theodore 37, 119, 120, 123, 124, 126, 127, 134, 135, 198
Rough Rider 126
Russia 158
Rutherford B. Hayes Library 95

S

Sagamore Hill 119, 126
San Francisco 130
San Jose, Calif. 126
San Juan, Battle of 119
Seaman (coachman) 119
Secret Service 124, 127, 134, 137, 138, 139, 143, 147, 150, 156, 158, 160, 162, 175, 176, 177, 179, 181, 182, 185, 195
Secret Servicemen 135
Senate Committee of Arrangements 97
Sesqui-Centennial Exposition in Philadelphia 34
Seymour, Beldon 44
Scott, Walter 27
Sharp, E. Charles 162

Shaw, Mr. 18
Shaw, Samuel J. 56
Shelburne Museum 43, 44 99
Shelburne, Vt. 43, 99
Sheldon Museum 43
Sherwood Forest 59, 62
Shetland ponies 90
Shriver, Thomas 65
Small, J. H. 197
Smith, Mr. 46
Smith, Mrs. Harrison 48
Smithsonian Institution 82, 93, 123, 151, 168
Snyder, Frederick Montford "Monte" 162, 168
Soldier's Home 82
South Bend, Ind. 80
South Dakota 126
South Engremont, Mass. 113
Southard, Samuel L. 45
Southington, Conn. 127
Spain 20
Spanish-American War 119
Springdale, Ark. 158
Springfield, Ill. 79, 80
Spring Lake, N.J. 162
Stables
    Philadelphia 21, 31
    Mt. Vernon 18, 20
    New York 20
    Sagamore Hill 119
    White House 32, 37, 47, 67, 75, 80, 82, 83, 89, 101, 103, 111, 120, 123, 124, 130, 197, 198, 203
Stable boy
    Thomas 75
    Nicolas (French Canadian) 87
Standard Oil Company 175
Stanley, F. O. 116
State Department 198, 203, 204
Staunton, Va. 138
Stephen Decatur House 93
Sterling, W. C. 130
Stevens, Mr. 39
Stinchcomb, Officer 83
Stone Controls Inc. 156
Stone, Whitney 34
Stony Brook, Long Island 77
Stover, Mrs. 85, 87
Straus, Secretary 124
Studebaker Brothers, 80, 101, 106, 108, 112
Studebaker Corporation 168
Studebaker Museum 93, 108
Suffolk Museum 77
Sultan of Turkey 93
Summit, N.J. 156

T

Taft, Helen 137
Taft, Mrs. Wm. H. 134, 204
Taft, William Howard 127, 129, 130, 133, 134, 135, 137, 139, 204
Taylor House 41
Taylor, Zachary 65, 66, 67
Tennessee 47, 53, 192
Tennessee Centennial Exhibition 47
Texas 192
Thomas auction rooms 26
Thomas Jefferson Memorial Foundation 34

Thomas, stable boy 75
Thomson, S. John 197
Tichenor, M. H. & Co. 120
Tilton, Governor 100
Todd, Mr. 15
Tom, (coachman) 120
Towers Apartment 179
Treasury Department 82, 198, 203, 204
Trenton, N.J. 27
Truman, Harry S 171, 172, 175, 176, 177, 181
Trumbull, Senator 83
Truxton, Commodore Thomas 53
Tully, Miss 160
Turkey Point, Ontario, Canada 116
Tyler, John 59
Tyler, Mrs. John 59, 62
Tyler, Mary Lyon 62

U

U.S. Capitol 34, 45, 46, 48, 66, 97, 101, 103, 104, 111, 134, 175
United States Frigate *Constitution* 49, 53, 56
U.S. House of Representatives 47
United States National Museum 26, 27, 29, 91
U.S. Senate 171, 181
Updegraff, Representative 97
Utica, Ill. 83

V

Valentine & Co. 113
Van Buren, Martin 53, 55, 56, 86
van Rensselaer, S. 198
Varden, John 29
"The Varnum," Washington, D.C. 34
Vergennes, Vt. 44
Versailles, France 138
Vicksburg campaign 90
Vigus, Titus W. 57
Virginia 59, 62
Virginia, State of 18
Virginia House of Assembly 18

W

Walter Reed Army Hospital 179, 195
War Department 123, 130, 139
War of 1812 41
Warm Springs, Ga. 156
Warner, A. P. 123
Warren Commission 191
Washington, D.C. 32, 39, 46, 47, 55, 65, 66, 79, 80, 89, 91, 93, 99, 101, 108, 113, 116, 123, 130, 133, 147, 151, 153, 156, 162, 171, 189

Washington, George 13, 14, 15, 18, 20, 21, 22, 23, 24, 25, 26, 27, 29, 31, 32, 197
   Riding habits 21, 26
   Southern tour 25
Washington & Lee University 176
Washington, Lund 15, 20
Washington Mansion 18
Washington, Martha 15, 19, 21, 22, 24, 25, 26, 27
Washington Monument 66
Washington, Mrs. George Augustine 20
The Washington Post 172, 175
Waterloo Woolen Manufacturing Co. 113
Waterman, George H. 162
Waterman, George H., Jr. 134
Watson, George W. 78
Waverley, Mass. 139
Way, George 27
Webster, Daniel 69
West Point, N.Y. 89
Wharton, Anne 48
Wheatland 78
Wheeling, W.Va. 47
Whigs of Baltimore 47, 49, 57
Whipple, Colonel Thomas J. 75
White Company 130, 134, 139
White, Edward P. "Doc" 139
White House 37, 38, 41, 43, 47, 48, 55, 56, 59, 63, 66, 67, 68, 70, 73, 74, 75, 80, 85, 89, 90, 91, 95, 97, 98, 99, 101, 106, 108, 111, 113, 120, 123, 126, 127, 129, 130, 133, 134, 139, 147, 153, 158, 162, 168, 171, 175, 176, 185, 189, 191, 196, 197, 198
   Garage 147, 162, 197, 204
White, Rollin H. 130
White Sewing Machine Company 129
Willis Creek 66
Willis, N. P. 48, 49, 66
Wilson, Edith Bolling 137, 138, 143
Wilson, Woodrow 120, 137, 138, 139
Wirt, William 45
Wirton, Charles D. 75
Wise, Mr. 59
Wood Brothers 80, 91
Wood, Tomlinson & Co. 69
The Woodrow Wilson Birthplace Foundation 138
World War I 120
World War II 160

Y

Yalta 158
Yard, James 43
Yarger, Virgil L. 98
Youngren, Harold T. 172

Z

Zangara Guiseppe (Joseph) 155

PRESIDENTS AND VICE PRESIDENTS OF THE UNITED STATES

Presidents	Vice Presidents	
George Washington	John Adams	Apr. 30, 1789-Mar. 4, 1797
John Adams	Thomas Jefferson	Mar. 4, 1797-Mar. 4, 1801
Thomas Jefferson	Aaron Burr	Mar. 4, 1801-Mar. 4, 1805
Thomas Jefferson	George Clinton	Mar. 4, 1805-Mar. 4, 1809
James Madison	George Clinton	Mar. 4, 1809-Mar. 4, 1813
James Madison	Elbridge Gerry	Mar. 4, 1813-Mar. 4, 1817
James Monroe	Daniel D. Tompkins	Mar. 4, 1817-Mar. 4, 1825
John Quincy Adams	John C. Calhoun	Mar. 4, 1825-Mar. 4, 1829
Andrew Jackson	John C. Calhoun	Mar. 4, 1829-Mar. 4, 1833
Andrew Jackson	Martin Van Buren	Mar. 4, 1833-Mar. 4, 1837
Martin Van Buren	Richard M. Johnson	Mar. 4, 1837-Mar. 4, 1841
William Henry Harrison	John Tyler	Mar. 4, 1841-Apr. 4, 1841
John Tyler		Apr. 6, 1841-Mar. 4, 1845
James K. Polk	George M. Dallas	Mar. 4, 1845-Mar. 4, 1849
Zachary Taylor	Millard Fillmore	Mar. 5, 1849-Jul. 9, 1850
Millard Fillmore		Jul. 10, 1850-Mar. 4, 1853
Franklin Pierce	William R. King	Mar. 4, 1853-Mar. 4, 1857
James Buchanan	John C. Breckinridge	Mar. 4, 1857-Mar. 4, 1861
Abraham Lincoln	Hannibal Hamlin	Mar. 4, 1861-Mar. 4, 1865
Abraham Lincoln	Andrew Johnson	Mar. 4, 1865-Apr. 15, 1865
Andrew Johnson		Apr. 15, 1865-Mar. 4, 1869
Ulysses S. Grant	Schuyler Colfax	Mar. 4, 1869-Mar. 4, 1873
Ulysses S. Grant	Henry Wilson	Mar. 4, 1873-Mar. 4, 1877
Rutherford B. Hayes	William A. Wheeler	Mar. 4, 1877-Mar. 4, 1881
James A. Garfield	Chester A. Arthur	Mar. 4, 1881-Sept. 19, 1881
Chester A. Arthur		Sept. 20, 1881-Mar. 4, 1885
Grover Cleveland	Thomas A. Hendrick	Mar. 4, 1885-Mar. 4, 1889
Benjamin Harrison	Levi P. Morton	Mar. 4, 1889-Mar. 4, 1893
Grover Cleveland	Adlai E. Stevenson	Mar. 4, 1893-Mar. 4, 1897
William McKinley	Garret A. Hobart	Mar. 4, 1897-Mar. 4, 1901
William McKinley	Theodore Roosevelt	Mar. 4, 1901-Sept. 14, 1901
Theodore Roosevelt		Sept. 14, 1901-Mar. 4, 1905
Theodore Roosevelt	Charles W. Fairbanks	Mar. 4, 1905-Mar. 4, 1909
William H. Taft	James S. Sherman	Mar. 4, 1909-Mar. 4, 1913
Woodrow Wilson	Thomas B. Marshall	Mar. 4, 1913-Mar. 4, 1921
Warren G. Harding	Calvin Coolidge	Mar. 4, 1921-Aug. 2, 1923
Calvin Coolidge		Aug. 3, 1923-Mar. 4, 1925
Calvin Coolidge	Charles G. Dawes	Mar. 4, 1925-Mar. 4, 1929
Herbert C. Hoover	Charles Curtis	Mar. 4, 1929-Mar. 4, 1933
Franklin D. Roosevelt	John N. Garner	Mar. 4, 1933-Jan. 19, 1941
Franklin D. Roosevelt	Henry A. Wallace	Jan. 20, 1941-Jan. 20, 1945
Franklin D. Roosevelt	Harry S Truman	Jan. 20, 1945-Apr. 12, 1945
Harry S Truman		Apr. 12, 1945-Jan. 20, 1949
Harry S Truman	Alben W. Barkley	Jan. 20, 1949-Jan. 20, 1953
Dwight D. Eisenhower	Richard M. Nixon	Jan. 20, 1953-Jan. 20, 1961
John F. Kennedy	Lyndon B. Johnson	Jan. 20, 1961-Nov. 22, 1963
Lyndon B. Johnson		Nov. 22, 1963-Jan. 20, 1965
Lyndon B. Johnson	Hubert H. Humphrey	Jan. 20, 1965-Jan. 20, 1969
Richard M. Nixon	Spiro T. Agnew	Jan. 20, 1969-